Asking

Asking

Inquirers in Conversation

HARRY T. COOK

WIPF *&* STOCK · Eugene, Oregon

ASKING
Inquirers in Conversation

Wipf & Stock
An Imprint of Wipf and Stock Publishers
199 W. 8th Ave., Suite 3
Eugene, OR 97401
www.wipfandstock.com

ISBN 13: 978-1-4982-5611-7

Manufactured in the U.S.A.

In honor of the late Rabbi Sherwin T. Wine, friend, colleague and encourager, and founder of the Society for Humanistic Judaism

The enterprise of critical thinking and evolving belief founded on the objective data of experience is no vice. Proclaiming "I believe, I believe" repeatedly until it has succeeded in pounding the intelligence of honest doubt into pious submission is no virtue.

Contents

Preface

THE PURPOSE of this little book is to stimulate critical thinking in matters of religion and religious thought, both of which are very much a part of the world's intellectual capital and, in particular, of the Jewish-Christian world in the West.

The invitation to the reader is to start (or join) a conversation that should be taking place among people who want to understand what part Western religions, their histories and their literature have played in the development of Western civilization. The idea, further, is to treat that history and literature as historical and textual scholarship treats any history and literature, rather than as a bazaar of spare parts for the construction and maintenance of abstract philosophical and theological systems to support the apparatus of institutional religions' authority.

In the preparation of this book I went repeatedly to the store of research and analysis I have amassed over the last forty-nine years from the beginning of graduate school until now—much of it in the history, ideas, and provenance of biblical and extra-biblical texts that form the literary foundation of postexilic Judaism and Christianity.

I have eschewed what later I will call "inherited certainties" bequeathed to us by the theological system builders. I have taken text and history as I found them and have gone on from there to wherever they have led. I reject the ceremonial insincerity known in Farsi as *tagieh*, the sacrifice of truth to religious imperatives.

Because it was forged in those disciplines, what follows is probably not for those who want their cherished belief system restored like an antique. It is for those who are ready and willing to check their creeds at the door and enter into conversation with other inquirers. The enterprise of critical thinking and evolving belief founded on the objective data of experience is no vice.

Proclaiming "I believe, I believe" repeatedly until it has succeeded in pounding the intelligence of honest doubt into pious submission is no virtue.

I mention with thanks my revered teachers of English and Latin grammar and literature: Leonard Clayton Bailey, Muriel McFarland Neeland, John R. Young, and Joseph J. Irwin, all of blessed memory; my teachers of Hebrew, Aramaic, and Greek: Charles Kessler and Helmer Ringgren; and finally, the late George A. Buttrick and Paul B. Hessert who were my graduate school mentors.

This book could not have been published without the help of my long-time friend, Thomas A. Mackey, and the cooperation of the Society for Humanistic Judaism, 28611 West Twelve Mile, Farmington Hills Michigan 48334. David J. Sparrow, another friend of many years, was also generous in his support.

I am grateful to Emily Everett, a most excellent copy editor, for her work on the manuscript, her attention to grammar, syntax, fact, and clarity—as well as her cheery spirit and sense of humor throughout the process.

To live in close confines with someone who thinks he is an author and spends what must seem an inordinate time with his books must be, at the very least, trying and, at the worst, maddening. My wife of thirty years, Susan Marie Chevalier, has never once rolled her eyes in exasperation, has only supported me, advised me, and done a great deal of the editorial work on anything of significance I have ever committed to paper or PC screen. Her second-nature knowledge of how language works, and doesn't work, has been of invaluable help—but I thank her most of all for her confidence that in the end I could write something worthy of other people's attention.

Let's by all means keep the conversation going. E-mail me anytime at revharrytcook@aol.com and let's talk.

Harry T. Cook
Royal Oak, Michigan
December 31, 2009

About the Society for Humanistic Judaism

THE CO-COPYRIGHTER of this book, the Society for Humanistic Judaism, is much more than its name denotes. It is, by definition, a society of humanists, founded in the 1960s to be the organizing principle of a nontheistic alternative in contemporary Jewish life.

Its reach goes both deeply into Jewish tradition and broadly throughout a culture that has long since abandoned conventional religious beliefs and rituals. Although it may be that some of those beliefs are still held and some of those rituals are still practiced, they are largely held and practiced for their form rather than their content. They may be compared to your great-aunt's sterling and crystal, i.e., antiques worth keeping around for their historical value but otherwise beyond practical use in these times.

While the Society for Humanistic Judaism is organized to celebrate Jewish identity and culture, it does so in the wider context of a secular humanistic philosophy of life. To be a secular humanist is to embrace as of first importance the welfare of human beings in both the individual and collective sense. A humanist is concerned about his or her fellow human beings in the here and now. Because he is also by nature agnostic about such ideas as "god," he tends to locate the rubrics for living in a utilitarian philosophy which emphasizes the greatest good for the greatest number.

A humanist judges the moral worth of an act by its consequences rather than by an extrinsic mandate, as in a divine commandment. Hillel the Elder (110 BCE–10 CE), when asked for the whole of Torah to be summed up in a hurry, said, "What is hateful to you, do not do to your fellow. This is the whole Torah; the rest is the explanation; go and learn." That is consequentialism at its simplest. And any humanist, Jewish or otherwise, would embrace it.

My connection with the Society for Humanistic Judaism began in friendship with its founding rabbi, the late Sherwin T. Wine (1928–2007). Rabbi Wine crafted the original definition of secular humanistic Judaism as the leader of a suburban Detroit congregation in 1963. Today the movement is worldwide.

I was drawn to Rabbi Wine as a colleague by his clear-eyed appreciation of religious agnosticism, i.e, affirming the reality of what is known, pressing to know more but refraining from affirmation of that which is either unknown or unknowable. That kind of empiricism had long been at the root of my research, and of course it applies equally to Judaism and Christianity inasmuch as the latter is an outgrowth of the former and, as such, shares much formative language, literature, and philosophy with it.

For my contribution of a lengthy biographical essay to a 2003 festschrift[1] for Rabbi Wine, I was made a life-member of the society—a distinction I cherish for both sentimental and substantive reasons. It is a special bond in memory and a constant reminder that agnostic, secular humanism is a liberating alternative to the often stultifying existence of conventional religion. My research and writing has flourished in direct proportion to the proximity I enjoyed with Rabbi Wine and with those friends I have come to know in the society.

It is a privilege to share the copyright ownership of this book with the Society for Humanistic Judaism.

H.T.C.

---

1. Harry T. Cook, Dan Cohn-Sherbok, and Marilyn Rowens, *A Life of Courage*, The Milan Press (2003).

A Word about Method

ACROSS THE years from 1963 to the present and in a variety of learning venues—from a university chapel to a modest suburban parish—I have endeavored to interest people in intellectual exploration of the history and literature of Western religions, and, in particular, the biblical texts common to Judaism and Christianity. Beyond that I have tried to engage the same people in philosophical and theological reflection on those texts, their origins and historical context. That effort has been welcomed and appreciated by small groups of people in each of those venues. Such people demonstrated more than passing interest in learning whatever I could teach and whatever they were equipped to learn.

Plenty of my professional colleagues in ministry dismissed my efforts as "information mongering," urging me to tend to the "more spiritual" aspects of the so-called religious life, whatever those might be. I politely declined to take that advice and persisted in being a teacher and fellow learner with those I served.

Out of the classes I taught and seminars I led came a host of inquiries which begat further inquiries that took on a life of their own as group after group became more intense in their quests to learn and process more. Over the years teaching became the center of what I did as a parish minister. Part of my discipline was to track the inquiries and their follow-up questions against the day I might put them and the responses to them in just such a document as this. In an effort to augment the corpus of questions, I solicited via my online exegetical publications further inquiries. Over four weeks, 238 people responded. To keep this book from growing to unwieldy proportions, I combined questions of a like nature into one. No question was ignored or left undealt with.

In a second section I offer an essay entitled "Where Inquiries of My Own Have Taken Me" to which I invite response and challenge, as it is my desire to keep this online conversation going. A third section is a sample exegetical essay demonstrating how an agnostic secular humanist deals with biblical texts for the benefit of inquirers and those who must prepare homilies, sermons or lectures using them.

Introduction

As I scan the landscape of religious thought at the end of the first decade of the millennium, I find myself to be an outlier, a reluctant a-theist where "god" is concerned and an agnostic on most other theological matters considered settled by most Christian bodies. I recently retired from congregational work, having rung up forty-two years an ordained minister in good standing of the Episcopal Church—not exactly what you would call an organization of free-thinkers. Moreover, I had been for twenty-one years employed by an Episcopal congregation whose members are unremarkable for their religious sentiments, though one of them did ask my successor if he was "the kind of priest who believes in God." I guess I had taught them to take a dim view of inherited certainties.

It is only fair to acknowledge that when my first book (*Christianity Beyond Creeds*) appeared in 1998, several families left my parish in high dudgeon. The more curious fact is they had heard my sermons, read articles of mine that appeared in the public press, and took courses I had offered over more than a decade. So it must have been the systemization of my research in the book that prompted their anger. I must say their noisy exit left the congregation in a kind of extraordinary state of serenity from which, happily, we had not yet recovered at the time of my retirement. The philosophical and theological inquiries I helped to launch proceeded apace as my other books rolled off the presses and my occasional forays into public commentary continued to bring the curious into our midst.

I was able to say from the pulpit "I am an atheist in that I am not a theist" and there was scarcely to be seen the blinking of an eye among those in the pews. They got it. What I am certain they did not get and are in wonderment about still is how the church hierarchy so blithely ignored this heretic in its midst. A possible answer to that unspoken question is that the hierarchy is as unsure of the veracity of orthodox beliefs as it is vigorous in its continued promulgation of them. In a semi-playful way I teased my orthodox detractors by daring them to indict me before an ecclesiastical court on charges of heresy—and some of them did try but without success. Had they succeeded, not only would the sale of my books have improved, but the church would finally have had to tack into a stiff and uncompromising gale of common sense. My detractors would neither want me to enjoy the former nor would they themselves be able to weather latter. They know they would have to fall back on that thing called faith which one biblical text so optimistically calls "the assurance of things hoped for, the conviction of things not seen"—a rather weak reed in the wind, as it turns out.

It is with the phrase "conviction of things not seen" that I have had difficulties. I may have been born an empiricist, for since the years of reason flowered I have demanded to apprehend in some more-or-less objective means (sight, sound, touch, taste, or smell, and rationalized intuition) data that would lead me to be able to say that such-and-such a thing is so, is true, is real. By a combination of those means, I became convinced that my parents loved me pretty much unconditionally, and that, for example, either the sun moved across the sky or, as I later came to appreciate, Earth rotates on its axis, thus exposing successive tracts of its surface to the sun during a dependable period of 24 hours (by the arbitrary calculation of time).

No observable data yet exist that have enabled me to say with acceptable certitude such things as "God created the heavens and Earth," or for the righteous there awaits eternal bliss and for the unrighteous eternal damnation. That much religious literature sets forth such tenets a priori I will not gainsay. What I insist is that none of them can be arrived at a posteriori, which as near as I can tell is how most rational people decide on what they can rely as being real and true.

As the anthropological and archaeological record demonstrates, the phenomenon of religion in the human epoch can be traced to disparate sources. It seems clear that the worship of ancestors is an early source as succeeding generations, in seeking to control their societies, appealed to the received wisdom vouchsafed to them by dead elders. W. Somerset Maugham depicted one of his characters saying, "This is not so strange when you reflect that from the earliest times the old have rubbed it in to the young that they, the old, are wiser than they, the young, and before the young had discovered what nonsense this was, they were old, too."[1]

To tamp down doubt among younger members of the tribe or clan that such elders knew what they were talking about, adult members erected shrines to the memories of their predecessors by then unseen. It does not take much imagination to see how that process evolved into a full-blown worship of "gods," but worship with an agendum, viz., to exercise control over people in creating and maintaining some semblance of societal order.

As agriculture replaced the hunter-gatherer societies, communities began to take shape out of loosely related tribes no doubt requiring some organization, division of labor and even greater control than was previously needed. It makes sense to think it was at this point that a thing we might call priesthood emerged as the guardian of the memories and enforcers of the order derived from them. It seems that in a good many societies of ancient civilizations, priests were to some degree in thrall to military and political leaders—an association that would become all too common in later times.

Such a time is now as religious leaders, often self-appointed, stumble over one another to claim possession of exclusive truth.

1. *Cakes and Ale*, ch. 11.

Such efforts dovetail nicely with the hunger for certainty at the grass roots. It is said that angry young Muslim men are content to blow themselves up in terrorist attacks because they have been convinced it is the will of Allah that the infidel societies of the West or sympathizers of the West should be destroyed. The preachers on American cable television are just as certain that the god of the Christian Bible is speaking through them a set of inexorable truths that must be accepted by one and all to ensure their eternal salvation and to spare them eternal damnation. This contrasts dramatically with the idea of discovering within one's own experience those elements and strategies that have been successful in the realization of peace and security, and then putting them into practice as examples others might wish to follow because their desirability has been demonstrated.

As the alphabet and written language took hold in the societies of antiquity, there was bound to have been the setting down of laws and covenants, stories and liturgical texts. The provenance of each can no doubt be traced to the "memories" of early communities related to the wisdom of unseen, that is to say dead, ancestors. And just as dead ancestors morphed into "gods," so did the eventually written record of the law they developed, and that evolved in the lives of their emergent communities, become sacred writ. It fell, of course, to the priests to mediate the texts of that record and thereby to consolidate their power and authority. The text meant what the priests said it meant because the priests were, by virtue of their station, supposed to possess a kind of gnosis not accessible to the masses. One can draw an almost direct line from the priests of antiquity to the fundamentalist preachers of our own era, who, despite their denial of the validity of the office, amount to a Protestant priesthood whose members tell their congregations the Bible means what it says and says what it means. The Roman Catholic hierarchy, notably under the current pope, Benedict XVI, appeals through the church's magisterium to the authority of the Bible as the Word of God, by which it does not mean the biblical text is inerrant in speaking for god, but that the pope and the magisterium interpret its inerrant content infallibly.

Such interpretations of so-called sacred texts enabled the bloody Crusades, abetted the church's demonization of Galileo, fueled the Inquisition and its latter-day extension under Benedict (especially in his latter days as Joseph Cardinal Ratzinger of the Holy Office) and inspired the legislatures of several U.S. states to attempt to outlaw the teaching of evolutionary biology in public schools. The science on which the modern practice of medicine and surgery operate is being called into question solely on the basis that the long-accepted theory of natural selection and the science that has flowed from its exhaustive testing do not conform to sacred texts. An outfit that calls itself the National Council on Bible Curriculum in Public Schools (hereinafter NCBCPS) is pushing the use of courses that teach science with no mention of evolution and that claim the U.S. Constitution is based on the Bible.

What if the Constitution were based on the Bible? It would simply have as its basis another set of documents set down by human beings. But that is not how the NCBCPS sees it. If that organization's public relations initiatives can convince enough people the Bible is of something other than human provenance, the gullibility of those convinced will easily admit to the Constitution's origin being thus derived. Of course, the assertion that any or all documents of the Bible are of anything other than human origin is beyond ludicrous. Yet that claim is made in a fashion credible to millions of people every day by exponents of one fundamentalism or another.

I have found both amusing and helpful E.L. Doctorow's commentary on sacred texts in his 2002 Massey Lectures at Harvard[2]. He likened sacred texts to stories:

> The sacred texts of all religions based on Hebrew scripture have been communally amended, rewritten, commented upon, interpreted by rabbis, priests, imams, in order to transform

2. Doctorow, *Reporting the Universe*, 53–55.

religious apprehension into churches, unmediated awe into dogma, inchoate feeling into sacrament, brute expression into ethical commandment. But the authorship of God, through his intermediaries, is uncontested. And if a portion of sacred text is illogical, opaque, self-contradictory, bipolar, enigmatic, God in his authorial perfection is not to be questioned, only we, his readers, for our inadequacies.

Doctorow went on to say that after the Enlightenment and the advent of modern science, "Storytelling as the prime means of understanding the world was so reduced in authority that today it is only children who continue to believe that stories are, by the fact of being told, true. Children and fundamentalists." What, then, shall religious exponents say of their cherished texts if they cannot say of them that they are revealed and therefore beyond challenge? They can say that such texts are repositories of human experience, inquiry, investigation, and acquired wisdom; that many passages in them are possessed of great lyrical beauty and astonishing insight worth paying attention to and considering in the making of important choices and decisions.

Imagine the relaxation of tension and conflict in the world, were religious leaders of the various communities of faith to refrain from claiming absolute and exclusive truth for their sacred texts. The energy now spent in the aggressive defense of the content of such texts would be channeled into packaging it for display and vending in the marketplace of ideas. To those who would complain that such a strategy would be an open door to syncretism, I say sectarianism certainly hasn't worked very well. Let's try a new way. Peace is preferable to war, calm to conflict, intelligent discussion to fevered controversy, light to heat.

My advocacy of the next logical step will make readers think of a philosophical development that was au courant almost fifty years ago and arose from the research and writing of such scholars as Paul M. van Buren, Gabriel Vahanian, Harvey Cox and Thomas Altizer to name but four. The development was dubbed by the popular press as "the death of God movement." It was not a movement, and it did nothing close to writing God's obituary. The argument was that "god-talk" had become ever more difficult in the wake of the Enlightenment as the work of Copernicus, Galileo, Newton, Darwin and Einstein had pretty much dismantled the universe of antiquity. The further argument was that the Holocaust and other dread episodes of what poet Robert Burns called "man's inhumanity to man"[3] had rendered the "dear heavenly father" concept of god incredible. Van Buren, in particular, argued after the fashion of David Hume, that human beings might more sensibly focus their attention on what could be apprehended by the senses and subsequently submitted to reason, viz., each other and the general affairs of humankind, and seek therein cues to further consideration and consequent action.

The perils inherent in god-talk were not as obvious a half-century ago as now. As fundamentalists across the religious spectrum have turned up the decibel level of their claims to truth, Allah, Yahweh, and whatever god it is that Roman Catholic and Protestant Christians posit seem to be in competition with one another. Osama bin Laden and his followers invoke Allah in merciless acts of terrorism. American supporters of George W. Bush invoked a weird alchemy of theism and patriotism in support of the war of attrition in Iraq and in other ideological endeavors. The Christian Right invokes the god of the Bible in its battle to fill the U.S. Supreme Court with justices supposed to be supportive of conservative causes.

The trouble with god-talk of any sort is there can be no argument with it. When the late Jerry Falwell declared that the god he worshiped—and believed to be the only and almighty god—wanted a constitutional amendment to outlaw abortion, Falwell was appealing to an unseen source of authority above and beyond the abilities of investigation, research, and reason. When the Muslim fanatic speaks the name of Allah just prior to pulling the pin on his vest bomb, there is also no argument. Allah speaks, the terrorist

---

3. Burns, "Man Was Made to Mourn."

believes, ergo: the resultant blast. Hindus and Muslims cheerfully cut each other to ribbons over which of what's left of them will occupy some site considered holy by each, but blessed by opposing gods. This is no way to run a world.

Van Buren and his contemporaries of the mid-1960s advocated a moratorium on god-talk until those who would thus speak could get their semantic and philosophical houses in sufficient order as to be able to use language that would not be ludicrous in the face of commonly accepted reality. Dietrich Bonhoeffer was their muse in that respect. Paul Tillich, who died in 1965 at about the time van Buren and the others were publishing, had offered his own guarded version of god-talk. Tillich had written cleverly of what he called "the Ground and Source of Being," and was fond of answering the sophomoric question, "Does God exist?" with a stern "*Nein!*" When he used the word "god," Tillich generally connected it to his phrase "the uncreated creator." Following Tillich's lead, I crafted the term "source-orderer" for *Christianity Beyond Creeds* to account for the fact that there is something rather than nothing, and that much of what is gives evidence of sometimes exquisite order. Further than that, I was and am unwilling to go.

The trouble with going any further is that all too soon characteristics are attributed to a source-orderer which are anthropocentric and therefore reflective of whoever is doing the attributing, so that, for example, a white, male, middle-class attributor will cast "god" in his own image. And further, the attributor will miraculously discover that his "god" likes things the way he himself likes them. It is obvious what happens when the "god" of one cultural experience bumps up against a "god" of an opposing cultural experience. It is ridiculous on the face of it that human beings in the twenty-first century are at best debating, and at worst taking up arms, over what "god" wills or which of the several posited "gods" is the real one.

Van Buren and company were not wrong to have proposed a moratorium on god-talk. Their work, in fact, was brilliant. So why, after the 15-minutes-of-fame treatment the media gave it, did it fade from public attention? My hypothesis is that inasmuch as timing is everything, their groundbreaking philosophical work was pushed into the background by the simultaneous explosions of the civil rights and anti-war movements and the sexual revolution which had all America by the ears for most of the ensuing decade. By the time things settled down after Watergate, evangelical fundamentalism and the conservative movement in politics were in the ascendant with no tolerance allowed for the embrace of ambiguity and continued inquiry. Everything was by then in the answer mode.

The exponential growth of the mega-church movement in America and the even greater expansion of what Penn State scholar Philip Jenkins[4] calls "southern Christianity" in Africa, Asia, and Pacific Rim nations with its predilection to fundamentalism leave little room for the kind of no-holds-barred probing and bold questioning that the religious philosophers of the mid-1960s undertook. The perils of failing to probe and question are obvious, and this document is a call to resume that kind of work and to compete in the public square for attention to its fruits. In my gloomier moments I find myself thinking that, unchecked, religion uncritically examined could be the death of us all.

Since I am by birth and upbringing a nominal Christian and have a half-century of adult years of experience with its churches, I will approach the next step from that vantage. If I were a Jew, all other things being equal, I would be thinking synagogue or temple. If I were a Muslim, a masjid. However, as one culturally conditioned for better or worse by Christianity, I pose the question: "Might there be somewhere a church or congregation whose members would consider rethinking their raison d'etre to the extent that they would consider turning themselves and their institution into a center for critical thinking and evolving belief, setting aside theological and ritual convention to focus on what life's experience

4. Jenkins, *The Next Christendom—The Coming of Global Christianity.*

has been trying to teach us throughout the human epoch about how people may live in peace and security with one another?"

Would such a community, such an institution agree to announce themselves as "People of Concern," as opposed to that impossibly meaningless cliché "people of faith," concerned for:

- the creation and nurturing of local, regional, national, and multinational politics of integrity;

- the rebuilding and repopulating of decayed American cities;

- the encouragement of academic freedom, scientific investigation, and research;

- the fostering of a societal commitment to peace and economic justice;

- the nurturing of the arts, the humanities, and a vigorous press—each part of the essence of democracy;

- the continued guarantee of civil liberties, including the separation of church and state;

- the promotion of a rational approach to religion and ethics?

Such a religious institution, having abandoned claims to the possession of revealed truth, meaningless and divisive god-talk and sectarianism in all its forms, would glow like a welcome lamp in an otherwise shadowy twilight and perhaps have the effect of turning it into a promising dawn. It would be a temple rededicated to the amazing power and potential of reason amid the chaos of unreason that has so much of institutional and movement religion in its grip. Its life would be a celebration of the human capacity to use doubt creatively, of the freedom to question and analyze. If such a church had "saints," they would have achieved that status as skeptics, never being finally satisfied with the form of any question, let alone any answer to it. It would be a community of people bound in the kind of trust that not only permits but encourages discernment—and that not as a destination but as a pilgrim journey of individuals united for inquiry. Such a community from time to time would take decisions for announcement and action based not (or not alone) on the contents of some ancient tome, but from its rationalization of experience, including what can be inferred from history.

Such a congregation would be one of inquirers unafraid of any question posed in integrity with no expectation of an immediate or completely satisfactory answer. There may be such blessed venues here and there among religious communities, but I do not know of one that quite meets that standard. I know absolutely there are countless people who bristle with questions and earnestly desire to have them heard, pondered, and worked over until they are clear. Maybe then answers can be sought.

I spent forty and more years in inquiry rather than proclamation, entertaining, and working through thousands of questions with thousands of people. The questions I heard in the 1960s I heard again in the '70s and '80s and '90s and well into the first decade of the twenty-first century. What follows are a number of those questions and an account of how they were dealt with in a venue of critical thinking and evolving belief.

2

Inquiry and Response: The Conversation

Q: Isn't a religious leader supposed to be in the business of telling people how to have a relationship with God?

THE FOUR words that stand out as important in that question are "telling," "relationship with" and "God." So-called religious leaders do far better to engage those who look to them for wisdom in dialogue rather than to offer monologues declaring the truth of such and such a thing. It is true—or should be true—that such congregational leaders as imams, rabbis, ministers and priests ought to be thoroughly versed in the history and literature, not only of their particular traditions but others as well. Congregational leaders should be scholars at least at the journeyman level, giving some part of every working day to keeping current with the scholarship of their particular specialties and conducting ongoing research, not only for hand-to-mouth sermon preparation but for widening and deepening their understanding. Such immersion helps religious leaders avoid giving pat answers to questions. It helps them invite inquirers into the reading at some level and into eventual discussion of the question itself so that it may be framed in such a way to provide a path to discovering the answer, if one there be. My experience is that the question-framing exercise frequently gathers to itself more questions so that the process turns into a full-blown inquiry in which "answers" are soon seen as conditional or provisional and are actually tools by which the expanding question is sharpened. Often the "question" becomes to the inquirer and his or her mentor what a hypothesis becomes to a laboratory scientist, viz., the platform for significant investigation, testing, etc. "Religious leaders" do better to become mentors and enablers of that kind of question process, thus drawing the inquirer into longer term consideration.

The phrase "relationship with" implies the necessity of no fewer than two distinct and accessible entities, both of which can be apprehended at the very least by sight, sound, and touch. In more intimate mammalian relationships the olfactory and gustatory senses also come into play. The dictionary is always a helpful reference. The one on my desk defines "relation" as "an aspect or quality that connects two or more things or parts as being or belonging together." "Relationship" is defined as "the relation connecting or binding participants in a relationship."

It is utterly common and wise for human beings to seek to know as much as possible about the other before forming a significant relationship. Employers, for example, normally undertake a thorough investigation into the personality, background, and aptitudes of those they propose to hire, as well as their prospects for fitting in to an existing firm or enterprise. Those who assist couples in preparing for marriage or in the sorting out of other important relationships will urge and enable couples to know and to know about each other before binding commitments are made. It has become common practice for congregations whose polities permit them to select their own clergy leadership to do thorough background checks on their candidates, to interview them sometimes exhaustively, to probe their personality traits, etc.

Given what we know about the formation of relationships that are more than casual hookups, how is it possible to talk about "having a relationship with God"? Relationships do not just happen. They are formed by and through fairly complex knowledge each party has gained of the other. How does one obtain knowledge of an unseen, probably unknowable, unknown? Frequent answers to this question involve "reading the Bible," "praying," and "trusting."

It is supposed that certain human beings over time have encountered a god or two, e.g., Moses in the burning but not burnt bush (Exod 3:1–2), Elijah in the sound of sheer silence (1 Kgs 19:12), Isaiah more graphically in the Temple (Isa 6:1–8). On the other hand, the Evangelist John insisted that "no one has ever seen God" (John 1:18).

Modern psychiatry has helped us understand that claims to have "seen" or "heard" what is not otherwise perceivable by others may be signs of emotional or mental instability. Modern psychology has helped us understand that claims to have "felt" things, such as compulsions to "speak" in nonsense syllables and call it "divine inspiration," are signs of abnormality. That being said, one must seriously consider that a "relationship with" any god may not be possible—other than one a person fantasizes and carries on in an imaginary world, much as a child will converse with an imaginary friend. Which brings us to the concept of "god."

In the absence of observable data, it is difficult for a rational person to discuss "god" as imagined by the theologians of various religious expressions. To do so, and assuming one does, requires a suspension of the normal critical methods of determining what is real and actual. I say to you that the proverbial moon is made of the proverbial green cheese, and you reply, "How do you know? What proof have you?" And I say, "I just know." You say in return, "What about the moon leads you to insist it is made of green cheese?" In riposte, I say, "That's what I've been taught or what I've always believed." The blatant logical fault in my last answer means I have removed myself from the possibility of any rational discussion with you about the nature of the moon.

I have trouble distinguishing such answers from those laid out in the creeds of the Christian church, which are essentially pronouncements about the truth of things. The cardinal archbishop of Chicago, Francis George, put it this way in a Sept. 5, 2000, article published by the church's Congregation for the Doctrine of the Faith: "The [church] opposes religious relativism, which bases truth in personal experience rather than in God's self-revelation in history." George is known for his eight-word treatment of the church's core teachings: "The Creed is true. I preach the truth." What is "God's self-revelation," one might ask? Orthodoxy answers: "God's self-revelation is expressed in sacred scripture and church tradition as framed and interpreted by the hierarchies of bishops over time."

It is "personal experience," in fact, that most stable people use to determine what is true: "I see that it is not raining, nor does it look as if it might, and the weatherman does not forecast rain at all for the next three days. Therefore I shall not need a raincoat today." The locus classicus of that process is Charles Darwin's years of observation and analysis of natural phenomenon that led him somewhat reluctantly to lay out his theory of natural selection in his 1859 *The Origin of Species.* As had his predecessor in science, Galileo, Darwin endured much opprobrium for having published that which was clearly in opposition to what on the face of it the Bible seemed to say and which was extended by way of doctrine to the creeds of the church. Galileo lived out his last years under house arrest for his trouble. Darwin was simply preached against—and still is.

To return to the original issue of the expectation that religious leaders should tell their congregants how to achieve a relationship with God, we may observe that such a task seems not to be within the realm of the possible unless the leader and the congregant agree, with Cardinal George and many another authority figures, that the church's doctrines are "true." What may follow from that is a process of catechesis wherein the congregant will internalize the terms of the creed, accept them as being statements of truth and attempt to form the desired relationship with a god accessible only through that god's self-revelation that, in turn, is accessible only through what the church is and does—a process that will admit of no relevancy where the much-despised "personal experience" is concerned.

Q: A follow-up: If I can't establish that relationship with God—or "a god," as you put it—what alternative can you offer me?

None but relationships with human beings. Classic Christianity has made a deal of what it calls "incarnation," literally enfleshment. Following the philosophical poetry of the Gospel according to John (1:1–18), the church imagines the unseen deity, which John calls the Logos, or living mind of the universe, becoming human. What theologians have generally done with that concept is fixate on the unseen deity rather than the human being in the body and persona of whom that living universal mind is alleged to have expressed itself in time and space. Maybe the message of John's lofty poetry is that the human being qua human being is at the end of the search for ultimate reality, as Paul Tillich might say. For what do human beings seek in the ether of religious sentiment? Do we seek meaning? Do we seek answers to riddles posed or not yet posed? Do human beings seek "a relationship with God" because it is sometimes difficult to have fulfilling relationships with other human beings?

One possible way to slake the thirst for the "relationship with God" would be to work assiduously on the possibilities of establishing and maintaining mutually fulfilling and responsive relationships with other human beings, all the way from the most intimate to the more platonic; to seek to plumb the depths in other people's psyches, to know them, when appropriate in the carnal sense, but to know them as much as they are willing to be known. It is possible that with such potentially rewarding effort under way, "deep will call unto deep" (Ps 42:7) in ways that would seem as if one were attuned with the music of the spheres. The same John who gave us the gospel that bears his name is in one way or another, directly or indirectly, almost assuredly responsible for what is known as the First Epistle of John. In that document appears at chapter 4, verses 20–21 a possible biblical answer to the desire to have "a relationship with God": "Those who do not love the brother or sister whom they have seen cannot love God whom they have not seen."

Q: In spite of the eloquence of both scientists and believers regarding the "wonderful order" in creation, this is a deeply flawed world of storms and earthquakes and such diseases as cancer. How is it possible to believe in a perfect life in "heaven" after this one?

First, consider that there is as much disorder or chaos in the universe as there is order. We do not yet know very much about the phenomenon known as "dark matter" and even less about the concept of "antimatter." That vast ignorance hints at more disorder and chaos than can even be perceived or predicted by astrophysicists. Splendid and marvelous order is evident in such exquisitely predictable phenomena as Earth's tides, sidereal time and the plain fact (and mystery) of gravity. However, in reading more widely and deeply in the scientific journals that can be understood by nonscientists, I think we find a lot less talk about "wonderful order" than about the not-so-wonderful uncertainty that more and more knowledge brings. If by "believers" one means those who read the priestly version of the creation story in Gen 1:1–2:4a as in any way a true account of the appearance of life on Earth, then no wonder believers and even believers who are scientists speak of a "wonderful order." If the gods (*elohim*) found it "very good," how could it be less than wonderful and who could say less wonderful than what?

As for the "deeply flawed world of storms and earthquakes and such diseases as cancer," how do we know these phenomena make Earth "deeply flawed"? Storms and earthquakes are produced entirely by natural occurrences on and over sea and land. Indeed, they sometimes have cataclysmic effects on human beings as well as other life forms upon which human life itself has dread effects. Why should not the wind be the wind, and why should not the tectonic plates of the still-evolving planets not shift as they do from time to time, thus altering the landscape above them on the surface of the earth?

The "Benedicite, omnia opera Domini"[1] celebrates the whole of the cosmic order as "all ye works of the Lord" are called on to

1. Book of Common Prayer 1979, pp. 47–49.

bend the knee to their creator. Winds, floods, frost, cold, lightnings, fire, heat, ice, and snow are included. The poet of antiquity who gave that song for the three young men to sing while sojourning in Nebuchadnezzar's fiery furnace knew well before Shakespeare that the flaws were not in the stars or elsewhere in the natural order but "in ourselves."[2] That is not to say that natural phenomena as earthquakes and violent storms are got up to punish erring humanity in whole or in part. It is to say that such natural occurrences sometimes catch human beings unawares or unprepared or defenseless, and human suffering is the result.

Of cancer, that most hated vermin of all, it is often said that it is the product of some as-yet undiscovered anomaly of cells gone wrong. Indeed, it may be, but the accursed thing is so pervasive among human beings that there must be something altogether natural about it, not unlike the monster sea storm or the ruinous earthquake. In any event, there has yet to appear a biological life form that does not have a more or less known "life expectancy"—a term that actually means "death expectancy." There is no living forever. Astrophysicists can even predict the dying of the sun and the implosion of its planetary satellites. All is in the process of evolution or perhaps devolution. That response is probably unsatisfying to those who really want to know the score, but what we're talking about here is life—life with all its pleasure and pain, good times and bad, certitudes and mysteries. The biblical counsel might be Ps 90:12: "So teach us to number our days that we may apply our hearts to wisdom," which supplication amounts to saying, "Help us keep in mind that we will none of us live forever, therefore help us further to live each day as fully and as usefully as we can."

The concept of "some kind of perfect life in heaven" that would presumably be envisioned as without end is so clearly a product of human longing and wishful thinking that it is astonishing that it is held out with such alacrity by some theologians and preachers. "Perfect" means "finished" more than it means "ideal"

2. Shakespeare, "Julius Caesar," I., ii., 134.

or "without flaw." "Heaven" is a loaded word—loaded, overborne with meanings the word does not have, at least as used in the Bible.

"Heaven" in Hebrew is *shamayim* (plural) and in Greek, *ouranos*. Both would be recognized by first-century CE speakers of either language as denoting not so much a space as an object or objects, such as a curtain made of muslin or hide stretched out between poles (see Isa 40:22, Ps 104:2) or a dome or hammered metal piece, as it were a mirror (see Gen 1:6, Ps 19:1). The New Testament Greek word commonly translated "heaven" has a meaning closer to the idea of a dome or firmament, the function of which is to keep the waters above Earth contained.

That said, we do understand that "heaven" has come to denote a place or state of being to which the real, essential self—or soul—is transported once the body dies. Is it necessary to say that the astronomy of Copernicus and Galileo and the mathematics and astrophysics of Einstein and the army of scientists who have followed in their train have discredited that concept of "heaven"?

A key to understanding the idea of "eternal life," that promise so often made in the New Testament and directed to those who keep the faith, is the very term "eternal life" itself. New Testament scholarship has helped us understand that the term does not denote any kind of metric, certainly not one of length. The term is more qualitative than quantitative. Hence, "eternal life" connotes the depth and breadth of an existing life—a life that while it lasts is invested in what matters, viz., the love of other human beings, the care of Earth and its environment, the pursuit of beauty in the arts and its enjoyment in nature. "Eternal life" means a life lived in such a way that one would wish it could be eternal. Its certain finiteness gives it special poignancy, which was the bit of wisdom the psalmist (in 90:12) must have captured in that phrase "so teach us to number our days."

Q: After listening to you all these years, I lost my faith in the resurrection of Christ. Where does that leave me with the church? If I can't say all that stuff in the creed about Jesus being raised on the third day, am I in trouble?

Let's talk about the word "faith." What do you figure "faith" is? It might help to know that the word in the original language of the New Testament translated as "faith" comes from a term for "trustworthiness." Its verb form in classic Greek was used by Thucydides thus: "to make oneself trustworthy" or reliable. One who had to lead others in battle had to be trustworthy, and he demonstrated it by his courage. Two key words there: "demonstrated" and "courage." One is likely to trust a person if that person demonstrates characteristics and qualities that cause another to rely on him or her. So "faith" in this sense means trusting a proven quality. The oft-used quotation from Heb 11:1—"Now faith is the assurance of things hoped for, the conviction of things not seen"—suggests that if one hopes hard enough for whatever, he can be assured of that for which he hopes, therefore he is convinced that the things he cannot yet see will nevertheless come to pass. My graduate school professor of Greek New Testament remarked once that the Hebrews quotation always made him think of a man on the rail of racetrack clutching his wager ticket in hopes that the horse he bet on would win. "It may be conviction he is feeling," the professor said, "but he looks like someone on the rack being pulled apart at both ends."

The terms we want to look at are "trustworthiness" and "courage." The only 100 percent certain thing about life is death. That is not a statement of pessimism but reality. One can "trust" in that. Not so certain is the possibility that one will love and be loved in ways that pass understanding and, in so doing and so being, will experience great heights of happiness and fulfillment. It is certainly difficult to imagine considering one's death being either happy or fulfilling; but inasmuch as death is certain for each and all, it is possible that one may choose to die for a cause or that his or her death may serve a cause. Some historians of American politics say they have come to see that the national trauma of John F. Kennedy's 1963 assassination helped pave the way for the passage of the Civil Rights Act of 1964—a bill that Kennedy had introduced just five months before the debacle in Dallas. President Johnson used the still-fresh image of Kennedy's Camelot to push the bill through a reluctant Congress. Martin Luther King Jr., who would be assassinated four years hence, is said to have remarked on Johnson's signing of the legislation: "John Kennedy's terrible death made this law possible."[3]

Few stable and charitable persons would wish another's death for any reason. That does not mean a death cannot be redemptive, as Dr. King said of Kennedy's. King's death had a redemptive quality in its own right. Both Kennedy and King stood and spoke for monumental changes in social custom and for laws to institute such changes in the nation's life. In so doing, they demonstrated courage. Neither knew what would be the outcome of their efforts, but they persisted despite the inherent dangers. King in particular was seen as trustworthy by his tens of thousands of followers. They marched because he marched. They protested because he protested. They practiced passive resistance because he practiced passive resistance.

Neither Kennedy nor King was raised from the dead, and no one expected or expects them to be. None of the New Testament narratives depict even Jesus' closest followers as believing that Jesus, having been executed, would return. The very first narrative about Jesus' resurrection comes from the Gospel according to Mark. It depicts certain women going to Jesus' temporary grave to prepare his body for final burial. They were so taken aback by what they saw and heard there that, the text says, "They went out and fled from the tomb, for terror and amazement had seized them,

---

3. The author was told this by the late Ralph Abernathy sometime in the early 1980s while Dr. Abernathy was en route to Albion College, Albion, Michigan, for a speaking engagement.

and they said nothing to anyone, for they were afraid" (Mark 16:8). So no one expected Jesus to be resurrected, and not a single New Testament gospel text says directly that he was. There are visions of him coming through locked doors and through walls of shuttered rooms. St. Paul says at 1 Cor 15:8 that the resurrected Jesus "appeared" to him.

The living images of John Kennedy and Martin Luther King abide among us still, long after their deaths. Those images moved people in new ways commensurate with the witness each had brought to the nation and the world. Neither, of course, has come back to life as reanimated tissue. But the aura of their personae dwells among us, King's in particular as his "I Have a Dream" speech has been bored into the nation's consciousness much in the same way that Lincoln's Gettysburg and Second Inaugural addresses have been. Politicians, community organizers, and just plain ordinary citizens have come to trust in and rely on the sentiments so eloquently laid out in King's utterances. They have, as you might say, "faith" in them. Few dare gainsay Lincoln's echo of Jefferson: "All men are created equal." Few dare quarrel with King's: "I have a dream that my four little children will one day live in a nation where they will not be judged by the color of their skin but by the content of their character."

So you say you are concerned about your inability and unwillingness to affirm belief in the church's creedal proclamation that Jesus was raised from the dead? Yet you have a pretty good grasp on what the gospels say Jesus was and was about. You know of his ethical wisdom (turn the other cheek, love your enemy, forgive infinitely). You affirm that wisdom and try to live by it because you consider it trustworthy counsel, and it gives you courage. You could say it lives in you and that you are striving to embody it. That's a habeas corpus. You have produced the body. Forget the creed.

ASKING

Q: Where did the idea that God wrote the Bible come from? Did somebody besides God decide what would be in the Bible?

The clause "God spake these words and said" frequently appears in biblical documents, and if one takes the clause at face value and trusts in the scribe who took down the words, it is not a long path to believing that God or a god wrote or dictated the contents of the Bible. You'd be surprised or perhaps even appalled at how many aspiring Christians hold that belief somewhat uncritically, but they are also quick to suppress the guffaw when considering the claim that Muhammad memorized dictation of Qur'an from the angel Gabriel in the early seventh century at some desert redoubt in Arabia. Or the similar claim of Joseph Smith that in 1823 an angel named Moroni led him to find the Book of Mormon inscribed on gold tablets that had been buried somewhere outside Manchester, New York. Why are these claims any more or less incredible than the one, for example, involving Moses and his tablets?

It seems fairly clear to the wider community of New Testament scholarship that the canonical gospels (Mark, Matthew, Luke, and John, along with several epistles mistakenly attributed to Paul) were given their authorial titles to add gravitas to their contents. Who would pay any attention to the Gospel according to Ralph? But to attribute them to those named within them as intimate followers of the gospels' central character (Jesus) would be thought to gain them wider audience. That device could have been and probably was used by other authors and editors of other biblical documents to add heft to their work. To quote God—as in "Thus saith the Lord"—was a kind of literary "Hail Mary pass" in hopes that people would give heed to the message.

It remained for the author (almost surely not Paul) of Second Timothy (chapter 3, verse 16) to declare, "All [literally 'every'] scripture is inspired by God." That leaves more questions than it provides answers, of course. The Greek phrase "inspired by God" is borne by one word: theo-pneusotos, which is notoriously difficult to translate. And "all scripture" (graphā) can mean something so simple as "every stroke of every scribe's stylus."

We would probably do well to acknowledge that some writing—as some paintings, some sculpture, some musical compositions—seem more inspired than others. You can listen to P.D.Q. Bach or Bach himself. You can read the funny papers, or you can read *War and Peace*. You can gaze on Manhattan subway graffiti, or you can go up to the Metropolitan Museum and view Renoir, Manet, or Degas. Clue? Their creators were each and all human.

As to the question of what's included or omitted from the Bible, the writer of 2 Tim 3:16 might have said God made such decisions by inspiring church elders and church councils to include this document and to exclude others. Where the so-called Old Testament documents are concerned, the inclusion issue was settled before the church set up in business, perhaps as early as 300–200 BCE, but no scholarly consensus exists on exactly when. Where the collection of the twenty-seven (more or less) documents of the New Testament are concerned, the question of inclusion-exclusion is a tad clearer. Elaine Pagels, in remarking on the Gospels of John and Thomas, points out that the church had, in effect, to choose between the "interpretation of God's presence on earth," Thomas having said "the light" was present in every human being, John saying it was present only in the incarnated Logos.[4]

We get some help in understanding how some documents got included in the canon and some did not in what the late John A.T. Robinson would later call "the primacy of John" and the diminution of the Gospel of Thomas from evolving Christian theology (to say nothing of its actual disappearance from the scene in the fourth century CE until its eventual rediscovery in 1945 at Nag Hammadi in Egypt).

The Council of Nicaea settled for centuries that it would be John's, not Thomas's, theology that would predominate. That was accomplished by promoting John and ignoring Thomas by not in-

---

4. Pagels, *Beyond Belief,* 40–41.

cluding it in the canon—along with such documents as the Gospel of the Egyptians, the Apocryphon of James, the Gospel of Peter, the Gospel of the Nazoreans, the Gospel of the Ebionites, the Acts of Pilate and other extant works. A little peek, for instance, into the Gospel of Peter will suggest why those who formulate the canon decided not to admit it. This is part of that gospel's account of the resurrection of Jesus: "They [the soldiers] saw three men come out from the sepulcher, and two of them sustaining the other, and a cross following them, and the heads of the two reaching to heaven, but that of him who was led of them overpassing the heavens."[5]

Thus we may say that who decided what would be included in the Bible were those who at various points had the authority to determine what would be considered canonical and what would not. They clearly took such decisions on the basis of what they believed and wanted others to believe. So blame it on the theologians who generally ruin everything.

Q: You have often stated in your writings that the Jesus of the gospels may be a composite figure. What is your evidence for this?

Referenced in the preceding section are the comments of Elaine Pagels concerning the competing appreciations of the messianic Jesus figure set forth by the authors of *According to John* and *According to Thomas*. A person approaching Christianity and its primary documents for the first time might well conclude that the persons or personages about whom John and Thomas were telling were not the same individual. Moreover, "Jesus" (or "yeshuah" as it would be rendered in the Aramaic of the period) was a version of "Joshua," a very common given name for Palestinian males in the Second Temple period and on into the first century CE.

Compare the Jesus who appears in Mark (the iconoclast) with the one who appears in Matthew (the fulfiller and fulfillment of the prophets) and with the one who appears in Luke (the univer-

5. Cameron, *The Other Gospels,* 80.

salist hope and fulfillment of Israel). Compare those variations on a somewhat similar character motif with the Jesus who appears in the Gospel of John—frequently the "I am" speaker whom John in the prologue of the gospel depicts not starting his life as a Galilean itinerant but as the Logos (creative force and wisdom) of God rendered into human flesh.

It is certainly possible to attribute the different and often competing portraits of Jesus that show up in the canonical gospels to the blinkered perceptions of various authors, as well as to the exigencies of the different communities living in different times and places in the late first century CE. Remembering that with the possible exception of Thomas, none of the known gospels was written or edited in anywhere near the form we have them before 70 CE—fully a generation after the events variously depicted in them would have occurred. It is doubtful that any writer or editor of a canonical gospel was living or old enough during the years Jesus is said to have lived (4 BCE to plus/minus 30–33 CE) to have known him (or them).

Add to that the growing understanding among some scholars of the New Testament texts (and include myself among those "some") that the gospels reflect more the needs and aspirations of the times and places in which they were assembled and that "Jesus" is almost a legendary or even mythical character in their pages. Whether that means "Jesus" was a composite figure or an individual differently perceived through the mists of passing years remains an open question. It took me many years to work out the hypothesis that Jesus might be a composite figure. I am still testing that hypothesis through research and analysis.

I happen also to be a cross between a dilettante and a low-level scholar of the fictional work of the early- to mid-twentieth-century American author Thomas Wolfe. It is often said that Wolfe's novels—more especially his first and best-known, *Look Homeward, Angel*—are autobiographical, that the characters we meet in them represent actual people in Wolfe's life simply given different names. That is true to an extent, but there are characters who come to life in their pages who are almost totally creations of the author. The writer of fiction appropriates qualities, characteristics, and mannerisms that he or she has witnessed in all kinds of people and turns them into qualities, characteristics, and mannerisms of characters that emerge from the authorial imagination. I have often thought that, to one degree or another, the gospel writers may have employed such a strategy in the construction of their narratives.

Q: Jesus told us to love our neighbor. That includes, in light of the parable of the Good Samaritan, even—if not especially—folk like ourselves. By that example, it appears we are to love the neighbor by feeding the hungry and tending to the sick. How does this square with the Paschal Lamb concept to the effect that his death paid for our sins? Is it more important to claim him as savior or teacher?

Let's start by saying that someone said to whom it may have concerned: "Love your neighbor." The word for "love" denotes passion only for fulfilling the needs of the other. It is a love that does not expect or require compensation. It is a self-abnegating love. The word "neighbor" means "the one nearby." The proximity issue was joined by Luke in the parable the inquirer has offered as an example. "Who is my neighbor?" the lawyer is depicted asking Jesus. The primary question was, "Which is the greatest commandment?" The answer was: Love God; love neighbor. You can't do the one without doing the other. Of course, the answer to the lawyer's question, "Just who is my neighbor?" was answered devastatingly with the well-known text: "A man was going down from Jerusalem to Jericho and fell among thieves." The story is the answer to the identity of the neighbor, meaning that proximity is not a metric of feet or yards or even miles. Proximity is being part of the human race, and one loves the race one member at a time wherever need makes itself obvious.

The "blood atonement" as a tenet of belief suggests a vengeful deity. There is certainly a sufficient number of biblical texts which, read uncritically, suggest the god of those texts is, indeed, vengeful, jealous, and without mercy. One is free, of course, to believe what one will, no matter how nonsensical or obnoxious it may be to those who believe otherwise or believe not at all. If, on the other hand, it seems to one that, considering the general drift of the gospel, how one deals with the fellow human being is the point of relating to the persona of Jesus, then Jesus' death is not as important as his life and his teachings.

Think about the impact of the speeches and acts of passive resistance in civil disobedience that marked the public career of the late Martin Luther King Jr. His assassination was a national disaster, to be sure, but when his birthday is celebrated each January 15, it is not the shot fired by James Earl Ray that we hear. We hear the voice of Dr. King relating his dream "that one day this nation will rise up and live out the true meaning of its creed: 'We hold these truths to be self-evident that all men are created equal.' "

It is not unreasonable to say that Dr. King's patient teaching and example had a salvific effect on the American nation. It not reasonable to say that his blood spilled by Ray's bullet saved anybody or anything.

The church has been handicapped over the centuries by the development of so-called "theories of atonement," beginning with the locus classicus of the genre in Jewish tradition as the scapegoat is cast off the precipice to its death, bearing the people's collective sin. The three principal ideas of atonement (reparation for wrongdoing) in the Christian tradition are "ransom," "substitution," and "moral example." In the first it is hypothesized that Christ's death paid a ransom to Satan to free humankind from perdition in his eternal company. In the second it is said that Son and the Father let a willing Christ be the substitute for the human race in the payment of death being, as Paul said, the wages of sin. In the third it is said that Jesus' moral example sets the standard for how one gets right with God—eternal punishment being out of the question, God being just. There are a number of variations on the general theme lurking about in theological tomes. Some of the biblical texts treating the atonement ideas are, e.g., Isa 53:3–12; 2 Cor 5:21; Gal 3:10, 13; 1 Pet 2:24, 3:18; John 12:27–33.

Q: Please distinguish between "believing" and "understanding." Which comes first?

Unfortunately, "believing" often precedes "understanding," and often enough replaces it. One does not wish her physician to "believe" a tumor is cancerous. One wants the physician to "know," to "understand" that it is and act accordingly. "Belief" as a word has a strange history of usage as in, "I believe in smaller government" or "I believe Jesus died to save me from my sins" or "I believe the global warming business is a hoax." Not a one of those "beliefs" is based on any understanding at all. One may favor "smaller government" because he prefers less rather than more regulation or a lower rather than a higher taxation rate. When belief in smaller government becomes a creedal tenet, the believer has moved beyond political science—if he was ever there to begin with—into the realm of religious certitude.

"I believe Jesus died to save my sins." "Really?" is about the only reply I am able to make to that kind of statement. If the believer is asked why she so believes, she is likely as not to answer, "Because that's what it says in the Bible." That, course, raises a whole other set of issues and questions. Suffice it to say, though, that the believer in this case has decided the passages in the Bible which she has read or been told about have given her warrant to believe a proposition that has no chance ever of being proven. No data of any kind exist to do so. The believer has chosen to embrace the idea perhaps out of wishful thinking.

"I believe the global warming business is a hoax." The believer in this case has bought the arguments of the deniers, viz., that melting glaciers, rising sea levels, severe drought in one place and severe storms in another, the migration of tropical flora and fauna to the subtropics, and those of the subtropics to the temperate zones, that mountaintops that were once covered with 100 centuries or more of snow are less and less so covered amount to fiction—the believer believes the whole business is a hoax and chooses to ignore and/or deny evidence that points in exactly the opposite direction. Thus "believing" can and often does traffic either in the unprovable or the preposterous.

"Understanding" emerges from the receipt of facts, their analysis, hypotheses based on them and their exhaustive testing. The desire for easy answers is frustrated by that ofttimes tedious one-step-forward-and-two-back process.

But can "understanding" lead to "belief"? Only if what is understood is based insofar as possible on known fact. It is not unreasonable to say, "I believe the sun rises in the east and sets in the west," because that's what all the data suggest—except, of course, the sun stands still as Earth rotates on its axis exposing different portions of its surface to the sun. The appearance and perceived disappearance of the sun, or the waxing and waning of its light, is so fundamental an understood phenomenon that "belief" in it or that it exists is well within the bounds of reason.

"Belief" in the salvific effect of Jesus' execution is a huge and impossible stretch for the mind to make. Try it this way: "I believe the death of my beloved cockatoo saved me from my sins." There is as much meaning in that statement as there is about the other. What are "sins" and why must one be "saved" from them? Saved for what? And so on.

Knowledge gained the hard way, as described above, over time yields understanding. If a belief proceeds from understanding, it will be a belief others who have examined and rationalized the data can share. On the other hand, a cathedral full of worshippers confessing as in one voice belief in "God, the Father Almighty," etc., does not pass the test I have just described.

ASKING

Q: What is to be made of the exchange depicted as having taken place between Jesus and a man who wanted to know what he had to do to inherit eternal life? The answer was, in effect, to obey the commandments. The man protested, saying he had already done that. Jesus said, "Oh, yeah. There is one more thing. Sell everything you own and give it to the poor." It is said that the man went away in sorrow because he had many possessions. This issue seems always ignored in sermons and Bible study classes. Why? Why has faith become the ticket rather than works?

The matter of divesting oneself of all personal property for the sake of total service to others—and presumably to answer some inner spiritual vocation—is something relatively few do. A homilist will not get heard if he or she insists that personal divestiture is the only way to be a Christian—not even if the homilist himself or herself has taken the vow of absolute poverty. Divestiture is itself a vocation. Some are inclined to it; some aren't. Having said that, how does one deal with the biblical text referenced in the question above? The answer is: like any other biblical text. It needs to be interpreted in light of what can be known of its context. The text suggests that Mark's vision of Jesus was as a provocateur, a tease even. He led on the man with his seemingly honest question and zapped him in the end with what would have appeared to him to be a work of supererogation. It wasn't enough that he trusted Jesus enough to ask him the $64 question about how to attain eternal life. Now it becomes necessary to give everything away to get it.

The question to ask about the text is: "How does it impact you?" Does one feel threatened by its uncompromising nature, e.g., do this or die? If everyone who came under the influence of the Christian gospel or the Hebrew prophets were to divest all, from whence would come the resources required to respond to the mandate of Matt 25:31–46: "When I was hungry, you gave me food"? Some one or some entity would have received the aggregate or part of the aggregate of the divesture or divestitures and therefore would have the opportunity to apportion it to those in need.

Perhaps the key to understanding the "sell all and give the proceeds to the poor" mandate is to consider the proposition that each and every human being by virtue of his/her birth has a claim on the resources of this world.

As to the faith-works axis: "Faith" generally means belief (minus supporting data) in such propositions that Jesus died for human sin but rose again, signaling the eventual resurrection for those who thus believe. Some branches of Protestantism insist one cannot hope for immortality absent the confession of that creedal tenet. The proposition is clear that such faith is a gift from God "lest any man should boast" (Eph 2:9). That passage insists it is by faith alone that whatever salvation is ensues.

The moral reputation of Christianity is saved by the Epistle of James, the author of which makes a persuasive argument that belief or faith is empty and of no effect without what he called "works," or, in the Greek, *erga*.

If the language of religion—especially God-speak—is metaphorical and refers primarily to the mind and emotions of human beings, then James' "works" would be considered as being a natural result of human thoughts and feelings. James spoke of such fundamental "works" as caring for the widow and the orphan—in other words, people who are powerless and without much recourse to justice, economic and otherwise.

Most expressions of Christianity slide from one side of the faith-works spectrum to the other in different times and places under different circumstances. Eventually, though, the question of relevance arises, and people ask why they are giving so much effort to believing this or that when they could just as well expend such effort on helping others.

Q: I am wondering when the church will get around to writing a new creed so that when we stand up and say together "We believe . . ." we will not be saying such things as "He ascended into heaven" or "He will come again to judge both the living and the dead."

It is helpful to remember that the creeds used in most confessional churches are, or are derivatives of, the so-called Apostles' Creed or the Nicene Creed, the former dating from some time in the second century CE and the latter from the mid-fourth century CE. In practice, the Apostles' Creed is proper to the liturgy of baptism as the candidate, his or her sponsors and the witnessing congregation affirm or reaffirm belief in the basic theological tenets of the church. Mostly drawn from scriptural sources, and so named because it is attributed to the second, more probably third, generation of Christian leaders, the Apostles Creed bids belief in an "almighty" deity responsible for the existence of "heaven and earth" (the fundamental realities posited in antiquity). Jesus Christ is named as that deity's "only Son"—"son" being a term known to the practitioners of other religions of the first and subsequent centuries of the Common Era as the human evidence of an unseen deity. The birth, means of death, and death itself, as well as the burial of the son, are referenced along with his resurrection, ascension, and certainty of his coming again as a judge of humanity. Finally is affirmation made of the existence of a "Holy Spirit" (the invisible and continuing presence of the creator and his only son), the church of which they are the mainstays, and finally the forgiveness of sins effected by the belief of the confessors, their resurrection to "Life everlasting."

That said, it is likewise important to acknowledge that the appearance of these so-called "creeds" were invariably the result of conflict. One of the earliest theological arguments that divided the first Christian communities to diverge from post-Temple Judaism was over whether the mystical figure into which Jesus had evolved was really human, or did he just "seem" to be human. Those who ended up thinking he had just "seemed" to be human were called Docetists, after the Greek *dokesis* (appearance).

The centrality of the personage of Jesus Christ in this creed is demonstrated by the fact that of its 113 words, seventy-four are given to account for him, while the deity gets a fraction of that (twelve words), the Holy Ghost gets all of six, and the existence of the church four (or eight if you consider that "the communion of saints" may be in apposition to "the church"). The forgiveness of sins, which would seem to be a prerequisite for "the resurrection of the body, and the life everlasting," gets four. It is the centrality of the messianic figure that counts most in this statement of belief.

By the time of Constantine the Great in the early- to mid-fourth century, the conflict had moved on from "the appearance of being human" to the literal composition of the messianic figure. Was he of one and the same substance or not? Was the Christ a creature like other human beings, or were he and his substance "deity"? The conflict was a major one that threatened the solidity of Constantine's widely dispersed and fractious empire. So the bishops were brought together in Nicaea (today's Iznik in Turkey) to decide which proposition was the truth of the matter. You can see their decision in the language of the Nicene Creed which is recited every Sunday and most holy days by Catholics, Anglicans and other communions around the world: ". . . We believe in one Lord, Jesus Christ, the only Son of God, eternally begotten of the Father, God from God, Light from Light, true God from true God, begotten, not made, of one Being with the Father. Through him all things were made . . ." It goes on to speak of his being born of the Virgin Mary, his resurrection, and ascension into heaven, etc. The Spirit and the church are affirmed, as are the baptism for the forgiveness of sins, the subsequent resurrection, "and the life of the world to come."

The question is, essentially: Why do Christian congregations in the twenty-first century continue to recite those texts 1,685 years after their composition out of an essentially political process as if Copernicus, Galileo, Newton, Darwin, and Einstein had not lived and done their epoch-making work in helping us latter-day human beings understand more fully the nature of the universe? It was in answer to that question that I published *Christianity Beyond Creeds* almost a dozen years ago and from which I quote here:

> The question is: How can the language of Christian belief be construed so that the data which first gave rise to its expression can be examined in light of the worldview by which we now interpret natural phenomena? Then may come the eventual reconstruction of the belief system which could make it and its terms credible and usable to people in our time.
>
> It is with that proposition in mind that I say the historic creeds of Christianity can no longer be used unexamined and without a new and responsible construction of their terms in Enlightenment language and concept. As they exist now and as they are commonly used, it is necessary to work around them. . . . If the Christian belief system is to survive as more than an artifact, if the centrality of Jesus is to mean anything beyond pious need-fulfillment, then our work is cut out for us. It is time to look with a critical eye at the creeds—anti-thought prisons in which the church confined itself willingly much too early in its life. . . . Creeds are attempts to define what is orthodox and what is not. Creeds are attempts to delimit belief in certain terms and to exclude from a given fellowship those who do not profess such creeds or who cannot profess every term of a given creed. If creeds could be thought of as temporary, "here's-where-we-are-now-or-were-then" statements and treated as open-ended and available to revision as those who continue to confess them come to new and different appreciation of what at first they believed, the creeds would be useful as points of reference—just as the light from stars long extinct can be seen today and used as astronomical points of reference.[6]

As to the idea of writing a new creed or creeds, it may be a better idea for the church to forgo them altogether, to live with the scriptural documents with their occasionally inspired texts and wisdom, and adopting for its life an agnosticism in matters that exceed the boundaries of accessible knowledge, a secularism that directs its energies and efforts to the here and now and a humanism that focuses those energies in the here and now on improving the well-being of the human race and its environment.

6. Cook, *Christianity Beyond Creeds*, 4–5.

Q: How is it possible to believe in "faith healing"? Is it really the issue of mind over matter? Was Mary Baker Eddy really right? And can prayer heal? Does God answer prayer?

From Aimee Semple McPherson to Billy Sunday to the array of faith healers all over cable television today, the fascination with "miracles" of healing has not abated. If you can take it, turn on your set at almost any hour of the day or night, and somewhere up and down the cable band you will find some earnest evangelist laying hands on the lame, the halt and the deaf—seldom the blind—and, voilá, they leap, they dance and they say they finally hear. Apart from a panel of disinterested physicians who would have fully examined them beforehand over time and attested to their various maladies followed by examinations after the laying on of hands, one could not credibly say they were healed of anything. Are such things faked? How could they not be to one extent or another? Perhaps "faked" is an unkind way to put it. There is such a thing as mass hysteria, and it can make a person do or not do almost anything if he or she abandons reason and common sense. I know a man who used to fly the New York-Washington shuttle every day and feigned a limp so believable that he was never suspected of cheating when he preboarded an open-seating flight. He told me once he found himself limping and even hurting when he was not shuttle-bound, so thoroughly had he convinced himself he was lame and in pain.

Might he have been a candidate for a "faith healing"? I asked him that once, and he said he would probably get rid of the limp and the occasional ghost pain the day his job changed so that he would not have to make the frequent round-trip. If ever he was "healed" in any sense of the word, his boss would have done it. Was it "by faith" or through circumstance? You decide.

Can prayer heal? That depends on your definition of "prayer." And that depends on one's philosophy of religion, if one has such a thing. Most Jews, Christians and Muslims are, at least in theory, theists. That is, their formal belief is in an actual deity that is unseen but thought to be powerful, maybe all-powerful as well as all-knowing, transcending the limits of space and time as we human beings understand them. On what data such a belief is based, I cannot tell. But a classic theist believes he can communicate with his deity through the medium known as prayer, i.e., by speaking to it out loud or silently or otherwise channeling its supposed presence. Some people actually say they hear their god speak back to them, if not in words then by some other means. Such people have been known to say they "felt" they received an answer to their prayer. Either they feel better than they did before they prayed, or something turned out to be what they prayed it would be or would not be. This is apparently data sufficient to say that prayer works.

Our English word "prayer" comes from the Latin *precaria*, which is derived from the Latin *precarius*, meaning "obtained by prayer" or "doubtful." It is directly related to our word "precarious," which means, according to the Merriam-Webster dictionary, "depending on the will or pleasure of another; dependent on uncertain premises; dubious; dependent on chance circumstances, unknown conditions, or uncertain developments; characterized by a lack of security or stability that threatens with danger." The dictionary suggests "dangerous" as the preferred synonym.

In my controversial book *Christianity Beyond Creeds* I said of prayer that it may, in communal form, be a kind of discussion in which the needs of individuals, the community and the world around it may be talked over with an eye to what the community can and should do. Such talking and listening, I wrote, can, if intentional and grounded in trust, prove to be a process of discernment, which, after all, is what prayer is supposed to be.

Intercessory prayer is particularly difficult to understand. Some years ago executives of a hospital in California owned and operated by a certain national church group decided to run a controlled experiment on the hypothesis that "prayer works." About 100 cardiac patients were, without their knowledge, divided into two approximately even groups. One group, again without the knowledge of the patients, was the subject of intercessory prayer that their condition would improve. The other group was ignored. The health of those in the first group improved markedly while that of the second group did not. Ergo, it was said, "Prayer works." There was much criticism of the experiment, mostly by cardiologists who did not practice at that particular hospital, and much of the so-called scientific evidence was called into question.

What was not discussed, however, was the nature of the deity to whom prayers were made or not made, and whether the prayers were willing to accept the possibility that their god would only do what they asked and for whom they asked it—calling into question just what kind of god theirs was.

Surely it is impossible to believe that the concept of a deity worthy of human attention could be seen as discriminating among the sick and granting blessing only to those whose sickness was brought before it in prayer. If it may be that there is a deity out there somewhere—or what Tillich would call a "ground of being"—aware and sympathetic, swell. If not—and we have scarce data upon which to posit the existence of such a deity—we need to carry on, drawing on the considerable resources of the human mind and emotions to ease suffering and give care and comfort.

But, as the inquirer put it, "Does God answer prayer?" To pray in the conventional way is to posit a personal god that can and presumably will hear the content of a prayer and perhaps in some discernable way respond to its petition. What observable or even inferable data can be put forward to suggest that such a proposition is more than a fantasy or wishful thinking? Indeed, one often hears the assertion that God does answer prayer. Just as often the person who avers that has just enjoyed a good outcome in a situation that could have gone either way. The outcome is credited to the intervention of the god to whom a prayer was supposedly addressed. When the outcome is not so good, the game answer is "Well, God knows best" or "It was God's will that . . ."

Try this experiment: Go into an empty room where you are certain no one else is present, where there are neither microphones, nor open windows, nor any chance of another hearing you when you speak. Then address the god whom you believe hears your prayers. Talk as long as you like, asking for as many or as much of whatever it is you desire. Then wait. Say that you have asked for $100,000 to pay off your debts, or that your terminally ill loved one will be pulled back from the onset of death and be miraculously healed. Wait for however long your patience lasts to see if either of those prayers is "answered" in a way any other person chosen at random would agree they had.

Assume for the sake of discussion that you heard nothing of a satisfactory nature, that a bag of cash did not suddenly appear, that your cell phone did not ring with the news that you had won the lottery, or that, upon inquiry, you learned that your loved one was all that closer to death instead of being on the mend. How would that alter your certainty that "God answers prayer"? The quid pro quo assumption implied in conventional petitionary prayer is that the prayer itself is one side of the equation and that what, if anything, is granted is the other. If "God answers prayer," then for every petition there must logically be a response. Silence does not count as that response.

Redo the experiment but change its terms. Go into the same room apart and use its quietude to collect your thoughts, to identify your various feelings about what is to you urgent. Think through what concerns you, sorting out as best you can fact from hope, need from want, and reasonable possibility from unreasonable desire. Along the way, identify as best you can how your acknowledgement of reality and reasonable possibility as to outcomes has made you feel. Own those feelings in a further acknowledgement that you are probably not in control of the dynamics of unfolding events; that, for example, your sister at seventy-six is in the active process of dying from an incurable, untreatable disease and that for what time she has left you might want to help her make peace with the assured outcome even as you are trying to do the same. Conversely, if it is that $100,000 you seek, try to figure out how you might marshal your skills and strength to obtain it, or some part of it, on your own initiative. Take what control you can to do what you desire and think you need.

Supposedly all that work you would have done in that room would have been done in your head over a period of time that might turn out to be longer or shorter than you would have imagined because you had lost track of time, so intent were you on dealing with your thoughts and feelings. Would that experience been any less efficacious for you than verbalizing petitions to an unseen deity of whose existence you are unsure and prevented from knowing in the way you know everything else? Can you now conceive of "prayer" as an interior conversation with yourself?

The problem with prayer in the cases where it is addressed to a deity presumed to be listening is analogous to a toy telephone that is connected to nothing beyond itself. All four of my kids at one time or another played with toy phones that would ring if the right button was pressed or the right handle turned in such and such a way. I have seen each of my children engage in animated conversations with people on the other end of the nonexistent wire who must have seemed real to them at the time. Perhaps the people at the other end were imaginary friends. Eventually children begin to answer and talk on real phones (sometimes at annoying length) with real people at the other end. When they grow up, they, like St. Paul, put away childish things and have real conversations. I have copies of the bills to prove it.

Q: The Bible says Jesus prayed, and He left us what we call the Lord's Prayer. If prayer is just a human exercise, how do you explain that?

You may not have realized it in the asking, but the question is less about prayer than it is about the nature of the documents known as the gospels. One does better not using the phrase "Jesus said" but

"The writer or writers/editor or editors of the document known as 'According to Mark' (or Matthew or Luke or John) attributed these words to one called Jesus." Not only is the identity of "Jesus" clouded by the varied versions of the character but by what the person or persons so called are purported to have said (and done), something very much at issue among scholars.

The two occurrences of what has come to be known as the Lord's prayer (Matt 6:9–13 and its parallel in Luke 11:2–4) appear more and more to represent very early liturgical texts—taken together, almost a formula or schematic for a liturgical recitation. In Matthew, the text follows the admonition not to make prayer a public spectacle to prove piety. It is preceded in Luke by the disciples' request that their leader teach them to pray as John the Baptist had taught his disciples, leaving the reader to wonder just exactly what the Baptist may have taught and whether, in Luke's imagination, what Jesus is credited with saying (in the Lucan text) is somehow a correction or comment on the Baptist's teaching. It should be noted there is a fragment of this at Mark 11:25 in which the forgiveness of trespasses is the only mention. That all three synoptic gospels make some mention of parallel or somewhat parallel texts suggests they were well-known in post-70 CE nascent Christianity and perhaps attributed to Jesus for the purpose of endowing them with authority.

All that said, it seems clear that what we call the Lord's prayer is more of a programmatic thing than the prescribed words of a prayer. The text really lays out a theological system. It fixes the unforgettable image of a male parent open to the petitions of his children—a profound theological tenet. It locates the "father" not in earth but in heaven; not here, in other words, but elsewhere in another realm—a touch of Neoplatonism perhaps. A quick reversion to Hebrew tradition ensues with the naming of that father "holy." Then back to Greek images again with the perfection of the heavenly realm invoked in the earthly one. "Give us today" is a forthright declaration that human beings are dependent on that "father" for daily sustenance. Then comes the humanistic plea to be forgiven wrongdoing in the same way that human beings try to forgive one another—almost a quid pro quo of bargaining. Penultimately, the text petitions the "father" not to put the pray-ers to too severe a test (presumably knowing they are but imperfect, of earth as opposed to heaven). Finally (only in Matthew) is the petition to be rescued from an evil and/or from one or ones that would lead one into an evil end.

Whether this text is a theist's prayer to an unseen deity or a humanist's exercise in meditation depends, of course, on the person using it. Whether or not a person named Jesus said it first and instructed his followers to say it as well is simply not known.

Q: I recently read a book by a scientist who said morality is impossible without some kind of religious foundation of belief. I used to be a believer, went to church and all that. I haven't been in years and don't believe very much, yet I still feel I am moral and have moral values. Am I off base here?

The issue you raise is by no means a new one. Philosophers and theologians have batted this one round for a long time. Perhaps the book you read was Robert Wright's recent *The Evolution of God*[7] in which he makes mention of the moral capacity of the human race which, in his opinion, has evolved along with humanity. As I read Wright, he is saying, in effect, that our moral capacity *is* the divine within us and that it (the divine, in lieu of a better word) is part and parcel of our evolution, helped along by natural selection that goes beyond biological traits and the urge to survive by adapting. It is possible, I suppose, to look out on those parts of the universe we can see or discern and construe what we observe as evidence of what some would call "the divine" or "god." It is also possible to look out in that way and see nothing of the kind. That leads such a philosopher as I to think that "god" may be not so much an element of evolution as a construct of the human imagination to

7. Wright, *The Evolution of God*.

help explain the otherwise unexplainable. It is not difficult to understand how and why human beings devised anthropomorphic images to account for their belief in a god or gods. Even the more sophisticated images as the ones we encounter in the Hebrew and Christian scriptures (burning bush, thin sound of silence, mighty rushing wind, etc.) are suspect as human inventions. Withal, among billions of human beings across a breadth of religious philosophies, belief in the existence of divinity persists either out of what some call unavoidable evidence or what others understand to be the demands of human need and wishful thinking.

John Calvin wrote that "the human mind [is] naturally endowed with the knowledge of God."[8]

But do what moral sense and sensibilities that find expression in human feeling, thought, and action have their roots or root causes in something other than the human being itself? And if it is believed that such sense and sensibilities have evolved, the question would be: From what? And how do we know that what we identify as "moral" did not exist in other forms in our more primitive ancestors? Who gets to define what "morals" and "morality" are? What kinds of human behavior inform such determinations?

The inquiry might begin with what students of nature have long observed as "the maternal instinct" as the female of a species seems to devote her life to the protection and rearing of her pups, her chicks, her cygnets, her goslings, her cubs, etc. To what degree human beings project on that observed animal behavior their own experiences as mother or child is not clear. It is as easy to anthropomorphize an animal as it is a concept of a god, or to call winsome kinds of behavior "moral." I have seen a male and female swan together break the neck of one of their cygnets and leave its corpse to float away to be eaten by a snapping turtle. I'm told by those who know that the swans' behavior was instinctive. As a human being I thought it cruel at the time.

As a member of a helping profession, I spent most of the last fifty years seeing human cruelty close up rolled out in a thousand

8. Calvin, *Institutes of the Christian Religion,* Vol. I. Ch. Iii.

examples of what would be thought by all but sociopaths to be immoral. I spent a lot of those same years involved in the civil rights movement and frequently found myself in argument with those who cited the Bible in support of segregation—of slavery, even—and consequent unequal treatment of African Americans. They saw nothing immoral in any of that, seeming satisfied, for example, that Bull Connor had turned the fire hoses and sicced the dogs on them, and thinking that African Americans, whom they called Negroes (or worse), demonstrated their innate immorality by disturbing the peace. "Why don't they just stay in their place?" was the question often asked me. Just as I through my own lens took the swan parents' behavior to be immoral, so I took the attitudes of those with whom I argued to be immoral. If the swans' behavior was instinctive, so perhaps were the attitudes of those on the other side of the race argument. Instinct in great part has to do with self-preservation. According to a marine ornithologist, the cygnet that was killed by its parents almost surely had some defect or injury that would make its continued presence with its "family" a danger to all of them. Those who saw law and order in Bull Connor's treatment of protesting blacks may well have been reacting out of instinct as well. There was much fear among whites in general during the mid-1960s that they might be overwhelmed if "they" took over.

So what is morality, and what is immorality? And if the former is connected in some way with a remote deity, with what is the latter connected? Contra Wright, I would say that behaviors we observe and that make us feel good about ourselves as human beings are probably those behaviors any of us would not mind having visited upon us. It's a kind of reverse of the "do unto others" formula. One might say, "The way Person A is treating Person B is really nice. Person A must be a moral person, and he or she can treat me that way anytime." Conversely, Person A may be treating Person B in a way one thinks is bad, and therefore immoral. It may be, then, that morality, like beauty, is in the eye of the beholder.

One of my earliest memories is of my father rushing through the front door and swooping my mother into his arms as she squealed. I was afraid he was hurting her and began myself to cry in distress. What he was actually doing was telling her that he had, at long last, passed the bar examination and could begin work as an attorney. How he was treating my mother had its roots in his own happiness and satisfaction, even as he shared that happiness and satisfaction with one he loved. Maybe, then, morality has its roots in love.

That, of course, leads to the next question: What is the source of love? That is the greater mystery. How is it that people can and will form relationships that endure despite "the heart-ache and the thousand natural shocks / that flesh is heir to"[9] and cause the individuals in such relationships to grow emotionally to the point that one would lay down his or her life for the other? With those last words, we are coming very close to language found in the New Testament and used of the Christ figure who is depicted as laying down his life in willing crucifixion to pay the cost of all human wrongdoing—that Christ figure already identified by the writer who used the "lay down his life" language of the deity in human form. See According to John 1:1–18. That theology, of course, falls under the category of hope rather than of fact. Crucifixion was a favorite practice of the Romans, which they had learned from the Persians and Carthaginians who honed the practice from the sixth century BCE. The Romans used it only incidentally as a means of execution, and death was not always the consequence. The idea was to expose a person to public ridicule by binding him with thongs and splaying him on cross pieces of wood. There were many cruel variations on the practice. Could it have been that a figure like the Jesus variously depicted in the gospels met that end? Probably. Could it later have been said of him that he laid down his life for his friends? Why not? That's how myth is made. Do true believers among Christians see the crucifixion, which they take as a fact of

9. Shakespeare, "Hamlet," Act 3, Scene 1, Lines 62–63.

history as told in the gospels, as a moral act? They do, indeed. If it occurred in any way that the gospels depict, it might have been a martyr's act of defiance, and it might not fall directly under the category of a moral act.

If what one does by way of interacting with another neither injures nor diminishes her, and if that act arises out of a conviction that the other is a center of freedom, an observer using our language would probably say the former is moral or at least not immoral. Can the same observer go on credibly to say that the motivation of the former is ipso facto a product of her religious belief? Probably not.

Q: Why do we think there is something, rather than nothing?

That is a perennial question for those inclined to think philosophically, and great armies of philosophers from academics to dilettantes to dabblers in the field have posed that question, often as a taunt. The trouble with the question is that human beings do not know what "nothing" is, except in metaphorical ways, if then. A bank account will have "nothing" in it and yet still exist. A coffee mug will have no coffee in it, being empty, but it is not "nothing." Nothing is the absence of anything, and human beings do not know what that is like. And if there were nothing, then we would not exist to ask why there is something.

The fact—and it is an enormous one—is that, as the poet wrote, "The world is so full of a number of things, I'm sure we should all be as happy as kings."[10] Meaning that the wonder of it all is staggering. Who would not want to know what ignited the Big Bang some 11.4 billion years ago, give or take several million? Who would not want to know why?

George Berkeley (1685–1753) was noted for his philosophy of "mentalism," in which the byword was *esse est percipi* (to be is to be perceived). If you cannot perceive it, it does not exist. It's a dif-

---

10. Stevenson, *A Child's Garden of Verses*, xxiv.

ficult argument to follow and even harder yet to refute. If you cannot perceive, say, nothingness, then for you it does not exist, and since no one can perceive nothingness (perhaps because it does not exist), ergo it does not exist. And how can you say anything about nothing existing when nothingness, could it be perceived, would therefore exist?

The answer to "Why is there something rather than nothing?" is therefore based on a false premise. The fact is there is a lot of "something," the origins of and possible purposes for which we barely understand, and then only in the light of a lot of speculation, some experimentation, and hypothesizing by scientists. The task may be not so much to ask "why" there is "something" but to seek to learn as much as possible about what it is.

Q: I remember from an intro to religion class I took in university the idea of "progressive revelation" that, if my memory serves me correctly, meant that the human race has been given or has discovered things over time that improve its understanding of God's plan. Does that make any sense? And how do we decide whose religion is superior in that respect?

The term "progressive revelation" as used in your question is a central tenet of the Bahá'í religion, which teaches that the one God has revealed to human beings the truth of life and the universe, mostly in the various known religions beginning with the Eastern ones, e.g., Hinduism and Buddhism, then moving on to Judaism, Christianity, Islam, and others on down the historical trajectory. Its followers honor all religions—they count nine in all and think of their own as if not the final revelation, the latest one. It is, of course, criticized for its syncretism, i.e., for giving each religion equal respect. The implication of the Bahá'í system is that the earlier religions, historically speaking, are less complete than the later ones where revelation is concerned, largely ignoring cultural and social factors that shaped the various belief systems. "Later is better," or at least "more complete," is a weak and indefensible idea.

For instance, it would be pretty difficult to improve on the eighth century BCE Hebrew prophet Amos' vision of economic and social justice ("let justice roll down like waters"[11]). Martin Luther King Jr. in the latter third of the twentieth century lifted it in its entirety from its 2,700-years-old context, and it worked perfectly.

The other use of "progressive revelation" in Christian theology refers mostly to the arbitrary division of the Judeo-Christian scriptures into old and new testaments, the idea being that a clearer image of the deity and the deity's law and will appears in the later writings.

A third use of the term is Darwinian in nature and has less to do with religious ideas than with the broader and deeper appreciation of nature that science has been providing in increasingly more sophisticated ways since the days of Francis Bacon, Galileo, Newton, Darwin, and Einstein. The scientific revolution and the Enlightenment that fed it and was enhanced by it enabled the human mind to expand its vision of nature and to look at the universe in different ways than religious texts had suggested.

In that sense, not only had life evolved and continued to evolve, so did human knowledge and understanding of it evolve as well.

As to the issue of different religions and their relative validity: If one is studying, for example, the Eastern religions and the Abrahamic ones (Judaism, Christianity, and Islam) in an attempt to decide which ones teach truth and to what extent, he will soon find himself in a world of conflict and confusion. Religions do not constitute a cafeteria. Individually they represent a culture or cultures whose evolved beliefs and practices have arisen out of their histories and been expressed to one degree or another in languages, dialects, and symbolism, in response to needs within a people's life, to crises, to natural disasters, etc. How one religion depicts a deity is likely to be different, maybe very different, from the way another religion in another culture, place or time depicts or depicted its deity or deities. What truth may be revealed in any study of any religion will have to do with the people whose religion it is, their

11. Amos 5:24.

history and development over time. The study of religions, then, is more a matter for anthropology than theology.

There is also the pragmatism factor. A religion may serve a utilitarian purpose for people of one ethnic group or culture when it may not for another. The teachings of Religion A will make perfect sense to some people and seem to others impossible. Likewise with Religion B. Thus do I recommend what in academe is called "comparative religion" as a helpful way to get at the question of "superiority." One semester in such a course will readily demonstrate that religions have some things in common but are as sometimes as different as a turkey is from a gnat or a dachshund from a German shepherd.

Q: I don't get what "spiritual" and "spirituality" mean. A friend says she is not religious but spiritual.

The common use of the word "spiritual" refers to a reality beyond (or almost beyond) the senses and the rational ability to process what the senses sense. For some, the word means something like a fourth dimension or a sixth sense. For others, it means an unseen realm in which deities with various names hold sway. Theists who speak of the spiritual realm believe the *theos* that dwells there— "there" not necessarily being a spatial term—has a maker-made relationship individually and collectively with the natural order and its many entities.

Mysteriously opened windows and slammed doors, auras, voices in the head, sacred images on tortillas, perceived noncorporeal presences, and the hunch that one is not alone when he is alone all add up to the popular sense of what spirituality is: It is belief in the supposed world of spirits. The Greeks had a great word for "spirit"—*pneuma*, meaning "wind." You can't see it or touch it or smell it. You can't really feel it, though you can feel the air when buffeted by it. "Spirituality," then, is active or passive participation in that unseen world which is, ipso facto, inaccessible to objective investigation and rational analysis. The term, as it is generally used, conjures up invisible and ungovernable forces that are beyond the powers of reason, and, therefore, wholly a matter of opinion. It is true that opinions are often embraced with great passion, which does not make them so. Spirituality is the soft side of theology or dei-ology of whatever god-talk one wants to use. It assigns to an invisible realm those things that are pronounced beyond intelligent discussion and debate. They become over time a priori givens that no one dares question.

More than a decade ago a search committee of a church was pursuing me to become its next minister. In the interview process I had pressed on me questions about how I would lead the congregation into "greater spiritual growth." I had to ask what they meant by "spiritual" and "spiritual growth." To a person, no one could quite say, other than, "You know, spiritual." One member of the committee said, "Well, you of all people should know." The committee had listed "spiritual leader" as its priority among credentials the new minister should have. The committee loved my other qualifications: excellent speaker, scholar, community organizer, engaging teacher, caring pastor. But I was told at the end of the process that another had been chosen because he promised "spiritual growth." It wasn't a year before he was on his way out, having few of the other qualities and skills necessary to the position.

I think I know what happened there. The members of the search committee, to a person, were well-educated—some of them academicians. Most were fifty and older and had been around the church in general and that congregation in particular for a long time. I think they knew the old faith was pretty much a dead letter and that the beliefs of former times no longer held much validity. They lived in a world they were having an increasingly hard time understanding and relating to, and thus found themselves in a vacuum of uncertainty. They were looking for a kind of balm to soothe them and hoped against hope it would come from their new minister, who would in some way be a guru to lead them into a new world still with the accoutrements of the old and the certainties that went with them. They knew I could not be that guru and so chose one who said he could. He disappointed them for one set of reasons as I would have for another.

The people of that church may also have been seeking empowerment. In an increasingly complex world, the individuals and subdivisions of communities of individuals tend to perceive that they do not have a great deal of power in and over their lives. The demands of society, of government, of day-to-day living sap strength, divert attention, and cause one to look at the details, no larger picture being visible. To be able (or enabled) to plunge into a warm bath of Reader's Digest-like platitudes and certainties can be an escape from that perceived powerlessness into a kind of magical world where the rough edges of troublesome concerns and issues, while no less vexing, become softer and more remote. Depending on what one does with it, such an experience may turn out to be more than mere anesthetics. It may call out from within an individual a Zen kind of determination to weather a storm, live with a disappointment, chart a different path, or even to turn suffering into poetry. Such things have happened.

There is such a thing as "secular spirituality," and it is that state in which people realize that things are not set in stone, and they can, are able to, mold their own futures according to their strengths, their aspirations, and the possibilities in the world.

Personally, I avoid spirit-type words, but in a gesture of goodwill and for pragmatic reasons they should be optional as long as it is understood that spirituality must be judged by its material fruits, the behavior of those motivated by it, and what it contributes to the good of the order.

Q: My minister says St. Paul was the founder of Christianity. His predecessor used to say Jesus was the founder of Christianity. Was either of them its founder? Who founded it?

Was George Washington the founder of the United States? Was Benjamin Franklin? Was Cotton Mather or Samuel Adams or

Thomas Jefferson? The answer to those questions is, "No." None of them was "the" founder of the country. Each was complicit in its founding, or, more properly, implicit and involved in its evolution from the days of the Jamestown and Massachusetts Bay colonies until this time and beyond. Whoever "Jesus" was—an actual person more or less as variously depicted in the gospels or, as may be the case, a composite character created out of several of a type of itinerant wisdom teachers who were active in Palestine of the early first century CE—he probably didn't found anything. He is depicted by the Gospel According to Mark as having appeared out of Galilee into Judea some time around 30 CE with a message that was as clear or clearer in his acts than in his words. The Gospels According to Matthew and Luke attempt to tell some things about the Jesus figure that clearly give off the odor of myth. The Gospel of John plunges right in, saying that Jesus Christ was the divine in human form. What the Jesus figure or figures as depicted in the canonical gospels represent is a line in time between the Judaism before 70 CE (the year of the Temple's destruction and the dismantlement of its priestly apparatus) and the emergence of rabbinical Judaism, and an innovative breakaway that came eventually to be known as Christianity and institutionally as the church. What seems to have happened is that collections of sayings (one of them could have been an early transcription of the Gospel of Thomas) attributed to one or more people called "Jesus" and compiled perhaps as early as or earlier even than 50 CE were circulated in Palestine and became the literature, supplemental to Torah and other Hebrew writings, of a movement within and around the Judaism of the period. The sayings are best understood as fundamental ethical wisdom, as in "turn the other cheek" (to one who has struck you) or "love your enemy" (as opposed to fighting him) or "give up your shirt as well as your coat" (to a destitute person).

The sayings ended up in one form or another in at least three documents we know of: the aforesaid Gospel of Thomas and the Gospels according to Matthew and Luke. New Testament scholars almost uniformly have come to the conclusion that the sayings have perhaps one common source which, appropriately enough, they call The Source, or in the German of early biblical criticism, Quelle, which in New Testament studies has been shortened to Q. One consensus is that the sayings, edited and adapted over time, became the impetus of a prophetic movement of the lower economic classes in early- to mid-first century Judaism and remained such until they were appropriated by Matthew and Luke (and in principle, it seems, by Mark) into the gospels that began to appear after 70 CE, in part, I think, as a response to the catastrophic event of that year.

The destruction of the Jerusalem Temple ushered in a new age for the Judaistic religions of Palestine. For the more traditional, it became a decentralized religion of the synagogues (assemblies) with the teacher-arbitrator known as the rabbi at the center of things. For the more innovative it became a movement centered around the various images of the various Jesuses of the gospels which in the three decades between circa 70 CE and 100 CE became more and more myth-laden, including interpreting Jesus' death as a sacrificial event instead of the martyrdom it probably was,[12] with almost believable narratives implying his resurrection and even his bodily ascension into the heavens. The gospels also included stories depicting Jesus performing miraculous healings. All this was catnip to those adrift in the post-Temple era while all around them the colorful spectacle of Graeco-Roman myth religions dominated the religious marketplace. But they had at hand in the evolving gospels a mythology of their own culminating in by the introduction to the Gospel According to John, which begins by linking the Jesus figure to the Logos of Greek cosmology and philosophy.

But that is only part of the story.

12. Crossan and Reed, *In Search of Paul*, 384: "Jesus did not simply die; he was publicly, legally, officially executed by the contemporary authorities of the Roman Empire, that is by the normalcy of civilization's permanent violence in his own time and place."

Saul of Tarsus, who took the name of Paul, emerged some-time in the 40s CE and held a very important place in the Judaistic religious sphere for the next twenty or so years, traveling here and there across what we call today the Middle East and Asia Minor from Jerusalem in the East to Rome in the West, spreading word of a different kind of religion with a Christ figure rather than a Jesus figure at its forefront. Judging from the corpus of his seven thought to be authentic epistles, Paul seemed less interested in the ethical wisdom attributed to the Jesus figure(s) and more interested in what that figure represented as the dying son of the Jewish god for the purpose of redeeming all humankind. Speaking of founding, it is fair to say Paul seems to have been responsible for the creation of communities of his brand of religion in such locales as Galatia, and the cities of Ephesus, Corinth, and Philippi. Much of his epistolary material concerns the life of and internal conflicts in those com-munities. Paul's theology is on major display in his Epistle to the Romans, the Galatians, and the Colossians. He proclaimed that "in Christ," by which he probably meant "within the community of those who understand Christ as the divine reconciler" (see Rom 5:6–10), there were no significant distinctions among human be-ings, "neither Jew nor Greek, slave nor free, male nor female; for all of you are one in Christ Jesus" (see Gal 3:27–28). Certainly Paul was a seminal figure in the evolution of the emerging Christianity in the Levant and on into Asia Minor, as we have seen.

Thus it is inaccurate to say that either Jesus (a figure shrouded in confusion between myth and history) or Paul was "a" or "the" founder of Christianity, much less of the church. They are person-ages writ large in the history of the evolution of the religion that finds much of its basis in the scrum of many ancient Near- and Middle-Eastern religions, the Hebrew bible, Graeco-Roman myth religions and in early Christian writings.

Q: How does the Christian religion and its creeds about "God the Father Almighty, Maker of Heaven and Earth" square with what we are beginning to more clearly understand about the beginnings of the universe and the evolution of life on this planet?

In 1995 the Hubble Telescope photographed a three trillion miles-long jet of gas traveling at millions of miles an hour—and that in one tiny section of space. Within that cloud it was thought that a star resided, which was then about 1,500 light-years away. Light from that star, could it have been observed from the surface of the earth, would be 1,500 years old—light that had left the star a few years after the fall of the Roman Empire. The farthest star visible in our galaxy is about 60,000 light-years away, meaning the light from it now perceivable left it circa 58,000 BCE, when Neanderthals still roamed across Europe. Simple cell life emerged about 3.8 billion years ago. As has been said earlier in this book, astrophysicists estimate the universe itself was exploded into being in a so-called Big Bang almost 11.4 billion years ago.

Even in terms of lofty poetry it is ludicrous in the twenty-first century to say that any or all of this was "made," much less by an unseen anthropomorphically imagined deity. The so-called Priestly writer(s) of Gen 1:1–2:4a (circa 450 BCE) used a Hebrew term that translates into English as "created," with a proper rendition of the verse being, "In the beginning of God's creating the heavens and the earth, God said . . ." as if the spoken word had caused to be assembled the parts of everything into the wholes as they would be perceived by human beings. Of course, the mid-fifth century BCE writer did not have the benefit of the Big Bang Theory, but with the image of "the spoken word" he was not far off in terms of symbolism. It seems reasonable to think some force ignited what the Big Bang became in the nanoseconds after its explosion and in ever more complex shapes and forms over the untold eons since.

The sole reason the religions that have sprung from the Hebrew bible have dealt theologically with origins is because theologians have mistaken the original intent of the Genesis passages as revelations of how life came to be. The first account of creation (Gen 1:2ff) represents a long and circumstantial argument for a Shabbat for postexilic Jews, whose leaders evidently thought that while they were in the business of inventing a religion and culture for themselves, they might as well, as it were, write into their constitution the setting apart of one day in seven for rest from the unremitting dawn-to-dusk labor necessary to living. The second (Gen 2:4bff) is an attempt to answer the everlasting questions about why things are as they are, whose fault it was that evil entered the human sphere. Once the sense of the "creation" narratives is understood, there is no point in adherents of Judaism or Christianity giving much time or energy to a creedal attribution of the world to their deity. Judaism and Christianity flower when the voices of the eighth-century Hebrew prophets and of the essential Jesus in the synoptic gospels are heard in their disquisitions on ethics and human behavior.

The scientific work of Galileo, Newton, Darwin, Einstein, and their successors has been and is being done quite apart from the creation narratives of Genesis and the creedal statements that proceed from it. The scientific community asks different questions than are implied in the Genesis documents' answers. Not that it will ever happen, but if this writer had his way, Christian creeds would be treated as historical documents, not as declarations of belief. At least the confession of belief in "the Maker of Heaven and Earth" ought to be heavily footnoted or dropped altogether.

Q: How can the doctrines of the Trinity, the Virgin Birth, the Resurrection, the Ascension, and the Immaculate Conception be given serious consideration by thinking people today?

"Serious consideration" can mean different things to different people. I give serious consideration to all those ideas when I see them depicted in oil paintings or sculpture of the Renaissance or in the texts of oratorios or motets. That doesn't mean I believe that what any of them depicts is true in a historical or journalistic sense. All the above-mentioned partake to a greater or lesser extent in symbolic language that reaches beyond its limited self to account for feeling. William Wordsworth wrote: "Poetry is the spontaneous overflow of powerful feelings; it takes its origin from emotion recollected in tranquility."[13] In that sense, I give serious consideration to the poetry in painting, music, sculpture, and the written word.

But is it possible to credit the literal truth of any of those doctrines you mention? It's difficult to see how. However, Roman Catholic clergy, in particular, and some of their theologians still insist they represent the truth in a very objective way. We must be content to let them do so in peace as long as they preach it in their churches and teach it in their seminaries. If they are taught in parochial schools to children and youths along with standard science, there is bound to be internal conflict of an intellectual nature, which is none of our business.

Perhaps it would help to take each of the doctrines one by one and seek to understand their origin in antiquity and usage in contemporary Christianity.

The problem with the Trinity begins with the noncontextual use of disparate passages from biblical documents in which the terms "Father," "Son," and "Spirit" or their cognates are used in different ways in different texts. Theologians over time systematized those references into a rigid, almost mathematical system, complete with graphics indicating that God is Father, Son, and Spirit, while Father is neither Son nor Spirit, the Son neither Father nor Spirit and the Spirit neither Father nor Son. Got it? The Nicene controversy over the nature of Christ (whether he was of the same or similar "substance" with the Father) exacerbated the debate, making it ever more nonsensical. The idea became that God was so unfathomable that the sparse monotheism of the Hebrew scripture could not begin to comprehend the idea and that the deity must be apprehended according to its various ministrations, e.g., cre-

13. Wordsworth, *Lyrical Ballads*.

ation, redemption and sanctification, but only as Three Persons in One. By the mid-eighteenth and early-nineteenth centuries, philosophers of religion, spurred on by the scientific revolution and the Enlightenment, began to abandon the doctrine as impossible intellectually and, failing to cross the bridge all the way, fell back on a monotheism of sorts that became known as Unitarianism, which, as near as I can tell, is best known by what it doesn't believe. Try not to say "Jesus" (except as an intentional blasphemy) in a Unitarian church. One of my theology professors in graduate school insisted that the Doctrine of the Trinity was the sole piece of the theological puzzle that gave Christianity its distinction. "Do away with it," he said, "and all is lost." I remember one of my classmates asking, "All what?" I wrote down in my notes from that day's lecture that the professor, a British Methodist, turned beet red and left the room, not forgetting to close the door behind him.

The Doctrine of the Virgin Birth is easier to explain but just as hard to live with. It begins with Isa 7:14: "Therefore Yahweh himself will give you a sign. Look, the young woman (*almah* in Hebrew) is with child and she shall bear a son, and shall name him Immanuel." When Isaiah was translated into the Greek of the Septuagint, the Hebrew *almah* (young woman of marriageable age) came out as the Greek *parthenos*, the usual translation of which is "virgin." At Matt 1:23 the Hebrew of Isa 7:14 is quoted and *almah* becomes *parthenos*, likewise in Luke at 1:27 and 34 where the unmistakable intent is to portray Mary as not yet having had intercourse (or lying about it). There is a debate among New Testament scholars as to what Matthew was up to. Did he know Hebrew, and did he choose *parthenos* on purpose to change what Isaiah said, or did he not know Hebrew and merely quoted the Septuagint? And was Luke simply following Matthew's lead either in ignorance of the Hebrew or in a deliberate tweaking of it?

Either way, once the theologians got their hands on these texts, they used them as evidence that the human being Jesus was born without biological assistance from a male. Such a claim was made for Octavius, eventually to be known as Augustus Caesar, and the Roman historian Suetonius took note of that claim in his "Lives of the Caesars" early in the second century. Moreover, Octavius was fond of being referred to as a son of god. It is not much of a stretch from there to the thinking of the first Christian theologians (I mean here in particular the authors/editors of the Gospels According to Matthew, Luke, and John) to portray the subject of their works in like manner. Luke did not help matters with a parenthetical aside at 3:23 in his reverse genealogy: "Jesus was the son (as was thought) of Joseph." There was no stopping the avalanche from that point on as the church headed into its imperial age, thence into medieval times. The fourth century CE was a definitive time as the Nicene Creed was formulated with the adoption of the theology of the Gospel According to John, which altogether skipped over the biological argument and went straight to the miraculous incarnation of God as Jesus Christ. Rational people in the twenty-first century will understand the doctrine of the virgin birth as a bit of theological history that is important to know about but not state as historical fact.

The gospels are in part carefully constructed arguments with the purpose of persuading people to believe what would otherwise be dismissed as pure fantasy. It is into this category that the doctrines of the virgin birth, as well as the resurrection and ascension of Christ, fall. As to the resurrection Easter, it is said Easter is the "queen of feasts," making the celebration of the resurrection the central theme of traditional Christianity. The resurrection is referenced in every creedal statement, including ones used conventionally even in the twenty-first century. It is said by orthodox theologians that the actual, physical resurrection of Jesus is the keystone of Christian theology, without which all is lost. It is said that Christ's rising from the dead was the divine validation of his ministry and, moreover, the triumph of good over evil, life over death and God over Satan. No rationalization accepted. No symbolism intended. It was a historic event and could have been reported on the front page of the Jerusalem Herald Tribune on that Sunday morning some 2,000 years ago.

If that were the case, then Jesus' resurrection would have been somewhat ho-hum news for that day. The Graeco-Roman myth religions had many dying and rising sons of the gods. No religion could be without one and have any chance in the marketplace of religions.

A close examination of some of the texts concerning the resurrection invariably leads the rational person away from the idea that it was a historic, reportable event. Mark, the first canonical gospel, leaves its readers with the sentence (referring to the women who went to Jesus' grave and found it unoccupied): "They told no one because they were afraid." Matthew and Luke both have guarded approaches to the idea. In Matthew a messenger of Yahweh descends to the gravesite to the accompaniment of an earthquake (the second within 48 hours, we are given to believe) and the two Marys going to the grave suddenly encounter one they took to be Jesus, leaving the gospel writer at this point to introduce the story that his disciples had stolen his body—a ruse to placate the authorities. Matthew has Jesus appear later to his disciples on a hillside in Galilee, though "some doubted," Matthew said. Luke tells a slightly different story: The women come to do the burial work and find two youths in white garments asking why they are seeking the living among the dead. The women go and tell all this to the disciples, who discount it. Later comes the matchless story of the deus ex machina appearance and disappearance of Jesus on the Road to Emmaus. (The Merriam-Webster dictionary defines "deus ex machina" as "a contrived solution to an apparently insoluble difficulty," the difficulty being in this case that the person in question was dead.) The Gospel of John is even more indefinite: Mary Magdalene encounters one she takes to be the gardener, but he speaks her name and she recognizes him as Jesus. Jesus tells her not to "hold on to him" because he has to "ascend" to his Father. Later John features three other mysterious "appearances" of a risen Jesus.

What one notices about all these texts is that none of them passes the eyewitness, corroborative account test that would be admissible in a court of law or able to be used as authentic by any journalist. If you are looking for such an account, try the one from the apocryphal Gospel of Pet 10:38–40 referenced on page 30. That is as close as we can get to an eyewitness account of a supposed resurrection, and it is not in the least credible, meaning that resurrection-speak must be understood as symbolic language.

As for the ascension of Christ, that, too, is a deus ex machina device. Once the evangelists declared a dead body reanimated in any way, they were required to grant a literary habeas corpus and produce the body. That they could not do, so it was left to Luke in the gospel at 24:50–53 and in the Acts of the Apostles 1:9 to depict the resurrected body rising further, this time from the earth in which it was supposedly buried into a cloud and thus out of the disciples' sight. The ascension is implied in Matthew at 28:16–20 but unmentioned by Mark or John. In John's account, the impression is given that Jesus in his risen form keeps hanging around (20:19ff and 21:4ff). So only for Luke did it seem necessary to complete the mythic portrayal by having Jesus reunited with his father in the place of honor with the right of succession. To insist in light of the observations of Galileo and Einstein that Jesus ascended into heaven is, of course, ridiculous. But it might be an elliptical way of saying that what his teachings represented and continue to represent is what one wishes the world to be like. It is to express the intention to live by those teachings and, by example, to persuade others to do likewise so that Jesus might be exalted in the lives of those who claim to follow him.

Q: Was Jesus married? Would any of the disciples have been?

Of course we have no way of knowing any of that, considering that the Jesus of the gospels is likely to be either a composite figure or at the least "remembered" differently by writers and editors who never met him. If there was a Jesus as he is portrayed by Mark and

Thomas in particular, he probably lived a rather ascetic life and may have had little time, energy, or inclination to take a wife, much less support the issue of such a union. As to the disciples, even less is "known" about them than about their putative leader. If any of them had been, as they are depicted, in the fishing business, it is a good bet they were married and with families as well. That may be the drama inherent in the passages that depict Jesus asking those who would follow him to forsake all but his mission.

In the marriages of first-century Palestine, as in most Mediterranean societies of antiquity, kinship was the key. Marriage occurred between close relatives, often cousins, through patriarchal connections having to do with economic concerns and necessities. The father of Jesus is referred to at Matt 13:55 as a *tektōn*, which approximately means "artificer," whether in stone, metal, or wood. Jesus is referred to as "the son of the carpenter" (*tektōn*). We are told nothing more. But if Jesus came from Nazareth, which rates no mention in the Old Testament, the Talmud or in the writings of Josephus, and must therefore have been a location of little significance, it is doubtful that anything other than subsistence farming took place there. *Tektōn* is not a far cry from *architektōn*, from which our word "architect" comes, both implying skilled labor and professional work. J.D. Crossan argues that *tektōn* could and probably did mean "day laborer." So any of the Jesuses about which the evangelists wrote would have been tied pretty closely to the work of subsistence farming and related chores and not out on the road, unless one of them was a neglectful husband, the suggestion of which I will leave to the "family values" crowd to parse.

Q: How can anyone continue to believe in a God of love when there is so much obvious, overt hate in the world? Why would such a God allow the Iraq war or any war?

An acquaintance who teaches history and philosophy at the undergraduate and graduate levels in Israel says Yahweh is "your basic son of a bitch," "a construct of emotionally unstable human beings," as revealed in the story of the near-sacrifice of Isaac (Gen 22). He says the idea of a benevolent deity turning a blind eye to the depredations of the Holocaust is "barbaric." My friend also says he is a tried-and-true Jew because "my grandfather was an atheist, my father was an atheist, and I am an atheist."

Clearly my friend does not begin his religious inquiries burdened by systematic or authoritarian belief systems. He spots in the texts that inform such systems evidence that the imagined deity is a product of conflicted human emotion. He says that one who knows the horrors of the Holocaust or of the Crusades or the fire-bombing of Dresden and Hamburg or the defoliation of Vietnam or the carpet bombing of Cambodia or the savage massacres committed on the orders of Pol Pot or the genocide in Rwanda and Bosnia or the invasion of Iraq or the murder of nuns and priests in Latin American banana republics cannot within the bounds of sanity affirm belief in an all-powerful and benevolent deity.

"G(g)od" is often an all-purpose word that speaks to the human desire to have a connection with origins more intimate than normal observation would consider possible. The vastness of what little, comparatively, we can know of the universe, its obvious disregard for human yearnings, the planetary food chain with the eater uncaring of the eaten all conspire to knock the wind out the idea of "God who marks the fall of every sparrow and numbers the hairs of every head" or that "God is love." If there broods over the universe any kind of intelligent force that would own up to being the source of life, one would passionately wish to inquire of that force just where the hell it has been over the eons as wanton and random violence has been as much a part of the picture as apparent order and predictability. Of course, it is a bit presumptuous to decide what is violence and what is order. The hawk circling its prey in tighter and tighter concentric circles, each one in a lower orbit than the one before, looks like order. When the hawk nosedives to just short of the earth and ascends with a stunned field mouse in its talons on its way back to the aerie with the hawklets' lunch, it looks like premeditated murder, unless you are a raptor who wishes you could be such an efficient hunter-gatherer for your own brood. From the point of view of the Amalgamated Field Mice Protective Association, what the hawk has done is evil. Of course, nature has its patterns, its food chain and its evolutionary aspect. The god of the hawk is in heaven, and all's right with that world, while down among the field mice it is wondered if their god doesn't care or whether it is powerless against the depredations of the hawk.

Whence the idea that the deity of the Bible is benevolent and "loving"? By conventional Christians it is said that the "loving" part is proven in the death of Jesus Christ, God's beloved only son—a divine life laid down once for all to atone fully for human sin past, present and future. As my Israeli professor acquaintance said with an ironic lift of an eyebrow, "It took Yahweh long enough. Where was he when the Babylonians were ravaging Judea in the sixth century [BCE], or Antiochus Epiphanes in the second?" In other words, as yet another acquaintance used to persist in reminding all around him: "S_ _ T HAPPENS."

Trying to place credit or blame on forces outside human experience for what happens within it for good or ill and then attempt to characterize a force as "good" or "evil" is an exercise in futility. One can justifiably blame much of the Great Recession of 2008–2009 on greedy, sociopathic bankers and financial speculators. One can blame 9/11 on the warped sense of political duty on the part of nineteen religious zealots. One can blame the rising ocean temperatures of global warming and the resultant weather extremes on the unsustainable habits and desires of human beings. Blame for none of these phenomena can in any sensible way be laid at the feet of an unseen, unknown and, for all intents and purposes, imagined deity.

In the First Epistle of John (4:8), "God is love." By "God" the writer meant the deity as imagined and worshiped by Jews and nascent Christians at the end of the first century CE. To back up that assertion, the writer refers to the argument above, viz., that God "sent his only Son . . . so we might live through him." The writer, possibly the same one as is considered responsible for most of the Gospel According to John, had clearly bought into the mystical aura that was draped around one or more actual human beings named Jesus and called "Christ," the anointed one. The rich irony is that, according to the myth, the death of Jesus was required to prove that love—the death being a quid pro quo atonement for human sin.

I have refrained from asking my friend, the Israeli academic, what he thought of such an idea. But I think both you, my reader, and I know what his reaction would be.

All this said, I would suggest that worrying about how a "loving God" can permit war or any other kind of action or event that seems on the face of it to be evil is a waste of intellectual energy perhaps better spent on asking how supposedly civilized human beings can permit war, etc.

Q: How can it be said that the United States of America is a Christian nation and should therefore reflect what are said to be biblical values?

It is undeniable that among the early immigrants to the American continent were people of the Christian persuasion—those in Jamestown of a more laid-back seventeenth-century Anglicanism, those of the Massachusetts Bay settlement of a more rigorous Protestantism. Both groups brought their religions with them, and instituted them in churches and assemblies. In New England, that religion's most noted exponents were Increase and Cotton Mather and Jonathan Edwards. The English immigrants, some by way of the Netherlands, entered upon territory that was already rich in various kinds of Native American religious spirituality quite unlike what had been imported. Such European missionaries as Father Marquette brought the richness of Tridentine Catholicism to the Great Lakes, founding missions here and there along the lakes and the rivers that emptied into them at frequent intervals. Lost, however, to all but dedicated and mostly obscure and neglected scholars and archaeologists is the sometimes spare evidence of Native American religion in the region. More is generally known about the religions of tribes of the far Northwest and Southwest. In any event, the land now called the contiguous forty-eight states of the United States was not "a Christian nation" to begin with or for a long time after. And when it became possible in a very narrow way to say it was, it had not yet acknowledged the presence of European Jewry here and there, mostly in the East. But over time, as immigration proceeded apace, America became more and more diverse culturally and religiously, until today one can drive along one stretch of a major cross-regional thoroughfare in suburban Detroit and within a few minutes pass or pass within a mile of Catholic, Episcopal, Presbyterian, Baptist and Methodist Churches, a Conservative Jewish synagogue, a humanist Jewish temple, Sikh and Buddhist temples and several eastern Orthodox edifices.

It is true that most of our Founding Parents were of the Christian persuasion. They could hardly have been anything else. Thus one would suppose that the Constitution of the United States of America would be replete with religious references to the Protestant Christian deity, etc. It is not. It conspicuously is not, meaning that its authors and signers clearly wanted to found a secular republic with the widest possible freedom of religion (see First Amendment). Thomas Jefferson sealed that deal with his famous letter to the Baptist ministers in Danbury, Connecticut, in 1802 in which he wrote: "I contemplate with sovereign reverence that act of the whole American people which declared that their legislature should make no law respecting an establishment of religion, or prohibiting the free exercise thereof, thus building a wall of separation between church and state."

What the First Amendment did was ensure a wide open opportunity for religious organizations of any and all kinds to set up shop where they would, preach and teach what was important to them and prosper if they could. No one could tell them what to preach. They were free to evangelize, even proselytize and otherwise recruit members to their ideology and cause. At the same time, implicit in the First Amendment is freedom *from* religion. It cannot in any form be forced on a resident of the United States. That's why in the early 1960s the U.S. Supreme Court ruled in several cases that the Constitution forbade the mandatory reading of the Bible or the offering of sectarian prayer in public school classrooms. It is why the American Civil Liberties Union is vigilant in suits against municipalities that persist in placing on public land overt symbols of Christian observances (e.g., nativity scenes) and has had to settle for an "equal-space" provision in which representatives of any religion may place their symbols on the same public land.

It is unclear what the phrase "biblical values" means, but to the evangelical fundamentalist Christian it generally means adherence to any statute of divine command that can be extracted from the biblical text, starting with the Ten Commandments and proceeding on through the entire collection. What in practice "biblical values" usually means is a set of public mores that do not make conventional Christians uncomfortable, that do little to change any societal status quo, that affirm a patriarchal arrangement in which men are the heads of households to whom all others in them must submit. I think it can be safely and truthfully said that America is not a "Christian nation" in its legal or cultural makeup, but that it is certainly home to millions of people who consider themselves by some lights to be "Christian," just as there are Americans who were born and brought up here who, for example, are self-consciously Jewish and Muslim—making America pretty much what the Founders envisioned: a land of religious freedom in which people are at liberty to believe and practice their chosen religions and in which people are at liberty to espouse or practice no religion whatsoever.

Q: If it is true that Jesus was crucified for what he had to say and his disciples were martyred for following his example, what idiot would follow his teachings?

Quite a few idiots, as you put it, have attempted to follow his teachings. Mohandas Gandhi comes to mind. He derived his strategy of nonviolent passive resistance from two teachings attributed to Jesus by gospel editors: "Turn the other cheek" (Matthew and Luke) and "Walk the second mile (upon being required to walk the first)" (Matthew). In so doing, Gandhi brought down the Raj and paved the way for Indian independence and democracy. Martin Luther King Jr. followed those teachings, always cautioning his more zealous followers to refrain from resisting in any but a passive way. The civil rights movement was largely carried along on his example. Your retort might be, "Well, both Gandhi and King were assassinated for their trouble." You'd be right. Such things happen, and both of them knew full well that assassination was possible in their futures, even as Jesus is depicted here and there in the gospels as foreseeing his own execution. The answer to that is not posthumously diagnosing them as having the martyr complex. For certain persons, the truth or right as they perceive it is of larger value than their individual lives. A well-trained soldier committed to the success of the unit will put himself or herself in harm's way to save fellow soldiers, sometimes at his or her own peril. Paul coined a phrase that appears in 1 Cor 4:10: "fools for Christ's sake." The saying came to mean acting sometimes in extraordinary ways to gain attention to a cause. So maybe when you used the word "idiot" you meant "fool." Some of us who manned the barricades on behalf of justice in the civil rights movement and of peace in the anti-Vietnam war movement were made to look like both idiots and fools by the establishment, whose representatives enjoyed putting demonstrators in jail or otherwise prosecuting them for disturbing the peace, as if beating up black people and destroying Vietnam in order to save it were not, both of them, egregious examples of disturbing the peace. But we took the abuse because we thought it was worth the witness it bore to those twin evils. Occasionally across the years, I felt like an idiot in some circumstances and like a fool in others, yet I would not now erase from the record those stands I took and how I took them, because the protests against the Vietnam war brought down one president, and the civil rights movement paved the way for the election of America's first black president.

Q: Can you give us a kind of time line of the Bible and what got written when?

It would be impossible to count the number of times someone has said to me, "I have read the Bible from the beginning to the end (fill in the number) times." My responses have varied over the years from "Splendid" to "Really?" to "I'm certain you did" to "Yeah?" I have sometimes said, "For your next marathon, why don't you read the Manhattan telephone directory from A to Z and see what you have learned?" I have tried to be kind, but patience has worn thin. Once in a while I asked the braggart if he or she had treated the public library in that fashion: reading the books from nearest the entrance to the back (auto repair to zoology) because that's exactly like reading the Bible (all sixty-six documents, more or less) in the order they appear. Yes, the word "genesis" is a translation of the Hebrew *b're'shith*, which means approximately "in the beginning" or "in the beginning of." But Gen 1:1–2:4a is one of the later written passages in the document.

The Bible is, as the German word *bibliothek* suggests, a library. It is organized neither according to the Dewey decimal system nor the Library of Congress scheme. The documents of what we call "the Old Testament" were assembled on scrolls, as one might see in a synagogue today. They are, variously, works of mythology (e.g., much of Genesis and Exodus); legal codes (e.g., parts of Exodus and Leviticus), Deuteronomy being a revised edition of much of what comes before it; stylized and often fabricated chronicles of the Jewish past; documents known as "wisdom literature" (e.g.,

Ecclesiastes, Job, Proverbs); hymnody and poetry (Psalms); what Jews call "the Writings," including what we know as the prophets (the three Isaiahs, Jeremiah, Ezekiel, Hosea, Joel, Amos, Obadiah, Jonah, Micah, Nahum, Habakkuk, Zephaniah, Zechariah and Malachi) who made their appearances as early as +/- 750 BC and as late as 535 BCE. The term "three Isaiahs" accounts for the more or less settled argument among scholars that the sixty-six so-called "chapters" of the document appear more or less in order of their appearance from as early as the 740s BCE to the 530s BCE. Second Isaiah (chapters 45–55) includes some of the document's more lyrical passages apparently written toward the end of or immediately after the end of the Babylonian exile (587–545 BCE). Daniel is probably the latest Old Testament document as it appears to have come at least in part out of the struggle and suffering in mid-second century BCE that Jews experienced during the pogroms of Antiochus Epiphanes circa 168–164 BCE. Six stories and four dream sequences give the document its distinctive apocalyptic character. Although the narrative suggests the time of the Babylonian exile, the tribulations of the late persecutions just prior to the Roman era were the historical material out of which the author or authors wrote.

One of the most helpful analyses of provenance in the Old Testament came in 1876 with the publishing of Julius Wellhausen's *Die Composition des Hexateuch,* in which he showed that the Pentateuch plus Joshua (later amended to include Judges, 1 and 2 Samuel and 1 and 2 Kings) had emerged over half a millennium from at least four disparate sources as far back as 950 BCE to as late as 450 BCE. One method by which Wellhausen, later joined by Karl Graf, outlined his hypothesis was to note the different names for the deity used by the different sources, leading him to give the shorthand name JEDP to his hypothesis:—"J" for the first letter (in German) of the name Jahweh, "E" for the first letter of "Elohim"(gods plural), "D" for the first letter in Deuteronomist (editor of the revised Torah) and "P" for the postexilic priests thought to have been responsible for much of the Levitical code. Dating the disparate sources is difficult, but the J Document could have been written as early as 950 BCE and reflects both truth and myth about the southern Davidic-Solomonic kingdom. The E Document from as early as 800–750 BCE is more associated with the northern kingdom. The D Document is thought by some to be "the scroll of Torah" supposedly found in the first temple by the high priest Hilkiah in 621–620 BCE, which spurred what became known as the reforms of King Josiah.

The twenty-seven documents known as "the New Testament" include the four canonical (i.e., accepted by the Catholic Church as authoritative as to binding faith and practice) gospels; as many as sixteen other documents can fall into the category of "gospel," most notably the Gospel of Thomas. Thomas, even though the discovery of its existence came as late 1945 CE and the version found is written in Coptic, may in fact come from as early as the mid-50s CE—fully two decades before Mark. Besides the four gospels, there is the Acts of the Apostles, which its author Luke called "the second book," the first being the gospel. Following Acts are, not in order of their writing, the epistles to Pauline communities in Rome, Corinth, Galatia, Philippi, Colossae, and Thessalonica. 1 Thessalonians is thought to have been the earliest Pauline letter and Philemon the last—all making their appearance approximately between 52 and 63 CE.

The Epistles to Timothy and Titus claim Pauline authorship but clearly are not, judging from vocabulary, syntax, and other hints obvious to scholars. Ephesians is thought to be a kind of encyclical or even cover document and was probably not dictated by Paul. The Epistle of (not to) the Hebrews is definitely not of Pauline origin and appears (and sounds like) a cross between a doctoral dissertation and a Supreme Court argument. It advocates primarily the perfection of Christ's sacrifice as being far superior to those made in the Temple, raising the interesting question of whether it is written before 70 CE, the year of the Temple's destruction, or after.

The Epistle of (not *to*) James is not exactly epistolary in nature once you get past the first few verses. It has more the earmarks of a tract. "James" was clearly a pivotal figure in early Jesus Judaism tending toward Christianity, but it is doubtful if the James mentioned as "the brother of the Lord" and as the patriarchal figure Paul says he went to meet in Jerusalem was the author of the document. 1 and 2 Peter are pseudonymous writings, certainly not composed by the mythical apostolic primus inter pares Peter. The authors of the two Petrine documents appropriated the name to give their ideas and arguments visibility and authority, not an uncommon practice in antiquity. 2 Peter may be the latest New Testament document.

The Epistle of Jude is of a similar ilk as 2 Peter, and, indeed, they share almost parallel texts (compare Jude 4–16 to 2 Pet 2:1–8). Jude is almost surely the "Judas" named in Matthew and Luke as a brother of Jesus. Jude's concern is best summed up in his most quoted line, "the faith once entrusted to the saints," and for his closing line at verses 24–25, a much used liturgical benediction even to this day.

Of the three epistles of John, which precede Jude, the first two are almost surely from the same author or his alter ego. While it was long thought that the author of the Johannine epistles was one and the same as the author of the gospel, a careful examination discloses that the John of the gospel did not operate in the kind of community revealed in the texts of the epistles. Much of the language and thematic content of the epistles is reminiscent of the gospel, which may be why their author(s) chose to use the name "John." A delightful surprise awaits the one who decides to give some attention to 2 John. Its opening line reads, "The elder (presumably the writer) to the elect lady and her children," evidence that women were important in the formation of the church. Third John is the only one of the three to be addressed to an individual (one Gaius). Others thus addressed are the Timothys, Titus, and Philemon.

Finally, the Revelation of St. John the Divine, perhaps the most misused set of texts in the whole biblical corpus. It is full of visions of last days, graphic and gripping imagery. It has been tempting over the centuries for biblical interpreters to take passages out of context in order to predict this or that cataclysmic event. Its prose and poetry were writ large in the now infamous Waco incident of 1993 when some 80 followers of religious fanatic David Koresh and their children perished in the Branch Davidian complex. Although Koresh reportedly leaned heavily on the imagery in the apocalyptic sections of Daniel, he made frequent references to the portents mentioned in the Revelation, so liable is it to misinterpretation and misuse by those who do not understand its text. The author of the Revelation seemed to have intimate knowledge of the Greek Septuagint. I count more than 250 allusions to Old Testament texts. Withal, its placement at the end of the Christian canon is appropriate, as in its own way it envisions the judgment and redemption of the world from evil forces both human and spiritual. The Revelation could have been written at the time of the collapse of Jerusalem or after but seems to reflect the kind of political conditions toward the close of Domitian's reign, circa 96 CE. Domitian insisted on being addressed as "Lord" and even as "God." Some of those had already decided that if a human being could be called by those names, it was Jesus Christ. For that they suffered persecution and even death upon their refusal thus to address or refer to the emperor. The Revelation comes to its culmination in the author's vision of "a new heaven and a new earth . . . and the holy city, the new Jerusalem coming down from heaven" in a time and place in which "death will be no more."

See the following general time line.

- 700 BCE 1st Isaiah, Amos, Hosea, Micah appear.

- 587 BCE Babylonian (modern Iraq) invasion of Judea. Judean wealth, aristocracy, artisans, brain trust exiled. Jeremiah appears.

- 545 BCE Persia (modern Iran) conquers Babylonia. Judeans expelled or freed, depending on how one reads the history. 2nd Isaiah, Ezekiel appear.

- 500 BCE Second Temple built. "Books of Moses" and other history formulated in which exile and return become slavery and Exodus. Ezra, Nehemiah appear.

- 333 BCE Alexander the Great dies, having created first modern super-state. Chaos follows.

- 166 BCE Zealous Judeans led by Judas Maccabeus declare they are mad as hell and are not going to take it anymore and act to restore the Temple and Judean tradition against the Alexandrian successors of Syria known as the Seleucids. One of them in particular—Antiochus Epiphanes IV—was the main scourge. The Maccabean victory is the legendary basis for the celebration of what you might call the Jewish Fourth of July: Hanukkah. Daniel appears.

- 63 BCE Pompey arrives in Jerusalem. Judea, Galilee and most of so-called "biblical lands" fall under Roman rule.

- 30 BCE Augustus becomes Emperor.

- 6-4 BCE Jesus born.

- 14 CE Tiberius becomes Emperor.

- 26 CE Pontius Pilate becomes Roman prefect of Judea.

- 40 CE? Saul of Tarsus switches sides.

- 41 CE Claudius becomes Emperor.

- 50–52 CE Paul writes 1, 2 Thessalonians.

- 53–54 CE Paul writes Galatians.

- 54–56 CE Paul writes 1, 2 Corinthians.

- 56–57 CE Paul writes his magnum opus: Romans.

- 58 CE(?) Paul dies perhaps in Roman captivity.

- 69 CE Vespasian becomes Emperor.

- 71 CE Gospel of Mark appears.

- 85 CE Gospel of Matthew appears.

- 95 CE Gospel of Luke appears*.

- 100 CE Gospel of John appears.

- 120 CE Gospel of Luke appears*.

* Some authorities argue for an early-second century composition for Luke

Q: Isn't the whole point of the Christian religion for its adherents to hope for and count on the hope of everlasting life? Why else would we try to do right if there is no long-term reward for doing so, when it is actually easier to "eat, drink and be merry for tomorrow you will die"?

Classic Christianity has been as good at painting a rosy picture of heaven as it has at portraying the eternal fires of hell. It has been fairly consistent in prescribing what a person needs to do to assure the former and to avoid the latter. That was part of the church's theology against which Martin Luther did battle, viz., the selling of indulgences to buy one's way some distance out of perdition. Luther's point, à la Augustine, was that God's disposition of grace toward sinners, especially repentant ones, was salvation enough. "For by grace you have been saved by faith, . . . so that no one may boast" (Eph 2:8–9). In such knowledge a person should be buoyed in a way that leads her to do the right thing, not to earn anything, but in thanksgiving for an undeserved gift. Paul, also in sync with that theology, observed in his Roman epistle that the point was not to sin so that grace may abound (6:1) "God forbid," he said. "How can we who have died to sin go on living in it?"

Your question no doubt arises from the concern that the images of both heaven and hell have been pretty much abandoned by rational people as places or states of being beyond life. Fear of death helped beget religion in the first place as people early on in their development as Homo sapiens acquired the ability to imagine beyond the moment or the day at hand, as human relationships became more sophisticated and spouses, parents and children and members of extended family began to experience the feelings of deeper attachment. Just as an infant cries for his or her mother, just as a child of tender years fears that mom and dad going out for a simple dinner date presages their never coming back, so did human beings begin to fear death as an irrevocable parting. They saw the inert corpses of those who had made that passage and knew instinctively they themselves were bound to end up that way. Wishful thinking may have been born at those kinds of moments. Inasmuch as dead ancestors were already revered as gods and would later be worshiped, one can see how the ideas, eventually, of immortality, resurrection, and reincarnation crept into the human psyche. That they did is not a sign of ignorance but of sophistication. The only trouble was that the scientific revolution came along in the seventeenth century and continues apace unto the present day, laying waste to any real hopes rational human beings may once have had of eternal heavenly dwellings. It was increasingly seen that death for human beings is as natural a phenomenon as it is for animal and plant life. Some one with a considerable IQ must have done the math and come to the realization that death was a necessary occurrence to keep the life of the planet in some kind of reasonable balance.

It is not vain to believe that the great human achievements in the arts—architecture, sculpture, painting, music, literature, and drama—were at some time in their inception and perfection intended to be self-created monuments to lives that would not last forever. So is Wolfgang Amadeus Mozart alive to this writer at this moment as over his computer's speaker he is hearing a rendition of the composer's Piano Concerto No. 2, K. 39, though he died 218 years ago. A casual walking tour through the galleries of any reputable art museum will make the artists come to life as will the serious reading of Milton's "Paradise Lost" or, say, Thomas Wolfe's *Look Homeward, Angel*. All those artists are long gone to nowhere but their graves. So is Mother Teresa of Calcutta. So are George Washington, Thomas Jefferson, Abraham Lincoln, Theodore Roosevelt, Franklin D. Roosevelt, Winston Churchill, Mohandas Gandhi, and Martin Luther King Jr., to name a few familiar personages of history. They live on, of course. The unmistakable visages of the first four named above loom over Keystone, S.D., to which more than two million people come every year to view them. The works of Franklin D. Roosevelt, Churchill, Gandhi and King live after them and will not be forgotten as long as the human epoch lasts.

In a smaller but no less significant way, how people help form, treat, and love their children lives on after them, too. It is what one does with his or life that matters. It is obvious that life generally doesn't last much longer than a century —a wink of an eye in the greater scope of time. "So teach us to number our days," said the poet who gave us the 90th psalm, "that we may apply our hearts to wisdom."

Q: Can you explain how it was that Judaism and Christianity became separate religions?

In fact, they are not separate religions but branches on the same family tree, that of the Semitic family of ancient Near Eastern religions of which Judaism is a relatively late refinement. Judaism's chief distinction among the others was its monotheism, i.e., the supposedly logical conclusion that there could really be only one deity. That sounds more benign than it turned out to be, because Yahweh (one of its names) was understood to be exceedingly jealous of so-called false gods and their worshipers who promoted them and the cults that grew up around them. The proscription of murder in the 613 commandments of Torah covered only those who worshiped Yahweh. Anybody else was fair game. In the medieval crusades, Christianity followed suit where Muslims were concerned.

The beginnings of what became known as Judaism may have occurred in the early thirteenth century BCE among the lower economic classes in cities along the eastern shore of the Mediterranean. These were largely economic oligarchies in which the very few possessed very much to the great disadvantage of the many. The masses had three choices:

1. They could work all their lives every day from dawn to dusk in what must have amounted to indentured servitude and accept their lot.

2. They could organize a rebellion with little chance of success, making their lot even worse.

3. They could up and leave.

The archaeological and textual records suggest that some number of them did, in fact, leave, migrating up into the hill country of what is now northern Israel and there establishing a series of small, egalitarian communities with codes of conduct intended to provide internal security against theft and murder by proscribing envy and adultery. Apparently they did not take gods with them as such entities would have belonged to their betters below in the cities. Eventually, though, the communities' codes included them, probably in this wise: As the first generation of the pioneer group died, the second generation found it convenient to keep the codes in place, as apparently they had worked pretty well. To do that it become necessary, as we might say today, to canonize the founders in some kind of exercises in ritual memory as in "Honor your father and your mother." As time went along, those memories became more and more faint and required a strengthening by positing the founders as deities, each community or federation of communities elevating its god or gods to supremacy as in "thou shalt worship no other gods but me."

The growing complexity of the lives of those communities and their eventual reorganization into a nation, and then nations, seemed to have required kings and priests and sacred writ including a "story" and, within it, stories. As in every emerging society, given human nature, there were certainly abuses of power threatening a return to the kind of economic conditions that begat the whole thing in the first place. Rising up to challenge that were public intellectuals called "prophets," the word meaning "those who name a thing for exactly what is," being truth-tellers. One such was Amos, a sheep tender and tree surgeon from lower Judea who somehow felt compelled to make what must have been a difficult overland journey to the seat of the king of Israel, Jeroboam II, there to upbraid him and his court for their treatment of the poor among them.

Over the subsequent 700 or so years, the emerging people known as Jews struggled through times of war and peace, subjugation, and success; were caught up in the whirlwind of the breakup of the Alexandrian empire; became wards of Rome, and so on and so on into the first century of the Common Era. The history of the Jews was hurtling toward a tragic culmination that occurred in 70 CE when Titus, a Roman general, mounted a siege on Jerusalem and demolished the central cultic site of Judaism, the Second Temple—the first having been done away with a little more than 600 years earlier by Nebuchadnezzar of Babylon. By this time a branch of Judaism had formed around the person of a Galilean legend named Yeshuah (or Jesus). Yeshuah, of which there may have been several of the type, was clearly in the tradition of the prophets, extracting and promoting the ethical content of the Jewish religion. Eventually his personage got mythologized at the hands of Paul and later John (the stated name of the author of the fourth gospel), causing the Yeshuah movement to diverge ever further from continuing Judaism, which itself became rabbinical Judaism following a different trajectory from the sect that evolved into Christianity and the church.

So, no: Judaism and Christianity are at bottom one religious stream of thought and belief, though culturally they have diverged over time. It takes practiced eyes and ears to appreciate the similarities that still exist. Liberal Protestantism has a natural and obvious connection to Reform and Secular Humanist Judaism, and its constituencies enjoy a generally amicable relationship. The more liturgical churches that take the theologies and mythologies of Christianity more seriously have less in common with Judaism.

Q: How do you explain the relative silence between the death of Jesus and the appearance of the gospels post-70 CE?

"Relative" would be the word. Of course, there were Paul's epistles (Romans, Corinthians, Galatians, Philippians, Colossians, and Philemon), all of which appeared from the early 40s to the mid-50s and reveal a sea change in Judaism as it was both before Paul's epoch-making proposals and before the destruction of the Temple in 70 CE. Paul saw the promotional value of recasting Judaism as a myth religion like the many that flourished in that part of the world at that time. His "neither Jew nor Greek"[14] sociopolitical stance suggests that he wanted the broadest possible expansion both ideologically and geographically of the religion he had inherited and was trying to reinvent.

During that same era, textual evidence found in the gospels of Matthew, Luke, and Thomas indicates there was another quite separate movement or movements centered around a collection or collections of sayings attributed to a Yeshuah (Jesus) that focused on ethics, i.e., how human beings can live in some semblance of peace and security. Examples are: Turn the other cheek, love enemy and neighbor alike, be generous in giving up what you don't need (or even *do* need) to one worse off than yourself, maintain a culture of forgiveness by forgiving as often as it takes, and (a riff on Hillel the Elder) treat others as you would yourself be treated. Those sayings plus a number of others in what some in New

---

14. Galatians 3:28.

Testament scholarship[15] have called "Q" or "The Source" appear sometimes verbatim or slightly altered in the gospels of Matthew and Luke and seriatim in the gospel of Thomas. It is reasonable to think that one of the divergences from ongoing Judaism during the first third of the first century CE were communities centered on the conservation of such texts and their promotion as a way of life. At the very least, their appearance in Matthew, Luke, and Thomas make it clear they existed before any of the canonical gospels and cannot have simply floated around in the ether until their incorporation in the same.

So there was not "silence" from circa 30–70 CE.

Shortly after 70 CE someone who took or was given the name "Mark" set down the first story version of the gospel, curiously not including so many of the Q sayings. But they re-emerge in Matthew and Luke, as we have observed, and became incorporated in their stories of miracles and other acts credited to Yeshuah together with various birth, death, resurrection, and ascension narratives. The presence of those narratives more or less follow the trajectory about which Paul was direct and specific, i.e., toward a transformation of Judaism from a law-based to a myth-based system complete with a dying and rising son of a god—the very stuff of which much popular religion was then made.

The various factions of continuing Judaism morphed into their rabbinical, synagogue-centered era as the sayings-of-Yeshuah groups got co-opted into the Pauline scheme with the Gospel of John still to come. John introduced into what would become Christianity the terminology and concepts of Hellenism, connecting Yeshuah, now called "Christ" (or the anointed one), to the eternal Logos, or creative intelligence of the universe which John insisted had become human in Yeshuah.

No, there was not "silence," but a gradual crescendo of theological noise, culminating in the primacy of John's philosophical vision over the ethical one of the sayings movement, thus result-

---

15. Mack, *The Lost Gospel*; Kloppenborg, *The Formation of Q*.

ing in an unfortunate cleavage between Judaism and its younger
sibling, Christianity.

Q: What if there is no God?

Ah, yes. But what if there were? How would you set out to convince another to believe in it? "It?" you ask. Why not? Why assume
that any deity will require a masculine pronoun—or a feminine
one? What kind of data would you seek to support an assertion
that there is a god? Is it the issue of causation that prompts your
question, as in what caused the beginnings of the universe and
its evolution? Or would you fall back on your reading of sacred
texts that purport to account for a god? Would you seek interpretation of such texts from authority figures such as shamans or gurus
or rabbis or imams or priests or bishops or popes, trusting that
any one of them would have knowledge that you would not have?
Putting the shoe on this foot changes the terms of the inquiry, does
it not? Mostly those who cannot quite summon up a belief in a
remote or unseen deity are put on the defensive to prove in some
way that there is no god. Try proving that there is.

Of course, either enterprise is doomed from the beginning
because evidence sufficient to demonstrate the existence or non-
existence of a deity such as conceived of in traditional terms is,
well, nonexistent. Thus the question is not, "Is there or is there not
a god?" The question is, "Why do we ask such a question?" Do we
ask it because we assume there is a god or that some numinous
presence broods over the universe or stirs somewhere in our mind
or emotions? Do we ask it because we have been conditioned to
believe in the existence of a god, or if not its existence, in its possibility beyond what we understand to be existence?

If there were a god, in what ways would we attempt to relate to
it? The adherents of most religions we know of practice some form
of prayer, i.e., attempts to communicate with the god in which they
believe, sometimes in an effort to persuade it to alter situations or
conditions according to the wishes of the pray-ers. Other forms of

what one might call prayer involve meditation or "listening" to the music of the spheres.

The English poet William Wordsworth wrote,

> And I have felt
> A presence that disturbs me with the joy
> Of elevated thoughts; a sense sublime
> Of something far more deeply interfused,
> Whose dwelling is the light of setting suns,
> And the round ocean, and the living air,
> And the blue sky, and in the mind of man;
> A motion and a spirit that impels
> All thinking objects, all objects of all thoughts,
> And rolls through all things.[16]

Wordsworth seems to have been writing of what others call "god," a sense, as he said, "sublime" and "deeply interfused," "a spirit that impels." He didn't say he "believed" it but that he "felt" it. In this poem, at least, he leaves the concept there: in the crucible of feeling, not imposing it on others but willingly conveying his own feeling for others to consider or not. He was not asking if there is a god or if the existence of a god should or should not be posited.

That is a really good place to leave the consideration about a "god."

16. Wordsworth, "Tintern Abbey."

3

Where Inquiries of My Own Have Taken Me: An Epilogue

THIS IS not a diatribe à la Richard Dawkins[1] or Sam Harris[2]. I am not angry, only frustrated and annoyed at how theism has for so long been allowed to cloud, complicate and trivialize the phenomenon known as religion. Religious historian Ramsay MacMullen[3] points out that well into the fourth century CE the title *theos* (God) "was fiercely reserved by a minority calling themselves 'Christian.' " Those who came to be known as Jews had at one time used the Hebrew term *elohim* ("gods," or "the fullness of deity"). *El* is considered by a consensus of most scholars of the Hebrew scriptures to be the generic pan-Semitic term for divinity—rendered in Akkadian, for example, as *ilu* and having something in each language to do with the idea of "power."

Thinkers in the ancient world must have had as much curiosity as Galileo, Newton, Darwin, and Einstein would demonstrate in much later times about how things worked and why they worked that way. People in antiquity certainly experienced "power" in the teeth of dust storms, floods, locust plagues, and death caused by what we now understand as infections. Since they were unable to locate the cause behind any of those, it was natural they should look beyond what they could see, hear, touch, taste, and smell to what they couldn't. Hence the idea of *el*, which served its purpose

---

1. Dawkins, *The God Delusion*.
2. Harris, *The End of Faith*.
3. MacMullen, *Voting About God in Early Church Councils*.

well in whatever language it was rendered until the time of the Enlightenment.

As god-worship developed as a philosophy of religion among Christians in a Hellenistic world, Christians came to believe that *theos* was an objective reality considered by some to dwell in a Platonic kind of perfect realm, who was, if not quite omnipresent, at least omniscient and certainly omnipotent. In due course, *theos* went from being remote to proximate to personal, so that theists would come to believe that "he" was closer than one's own skin, and not only "to whom all hearts are open, all desires known and from whom no secrets are hid,"[4] but accessible through the medium known as prayer and even open to manipulation through intercessory prayer to change the course of what was otherwise perceived as a natural process. It was not long before *theos* and "his" will began to be "revealed," especially to those who held high office in the Christian church. So now we know that *theos* finds homosexuality and its physical expressions offensive, that "he" takes a dim view of women in church leadership, that belief in the sacrificial death of "his only son" is the exclusive ticket to eternal salvation.

A bit more than a millennium into the Christian era, we learned that followers of Muhammad are the infidel and that "the holy land" must be reclaimed for Christ and his religion. This is the kind of thing that makes Dawkins and Harris foam at the mouth. It is the kind of thing that makes me determined to locate the religious impulse in agnosticism and ethical concerns.

A good beginning is to note that the word "religion" is derived from the Latin *religare*, which means restraint. Not so much to be restrained as to restrain oneself. Religion, therefore, is, semantically speaking, "restraint." One can see immediately the ethical aspect of the word. One is self-restrained from entering another's space for purposes of ridiculing, injuring, or depriving him of what is his. The idea of restraint goes as far as not denying by force or manipulation another's beliefs. There agnosticism is the key. One

---

4. *Book of Common Prayer*, 1979, 355.

can "know" for himself, but not for another. If as Sherwin T. Wine[5] said, a "religion is to be judged by the behavior of its adherents," then a religion that is unrestrained in terms of how its adherents behave (i.e., slaying the infidel, bombing Planned Parenthood clinics, suicide bombings) is not, strictly speaking, a "religion."

In each case named in the parenthetical part of the previous sentence, theism is the philosophical basis—belief that the *theos* is the only *theos* and that "his" intermediaries (hierarchs, scriptures, revelations) trump all in the determination of the truth. Take the organization known as Concerned Women for America, whose self-proclaimed mission is "to protect and promote biblical values among all citizens," the Bible being "the inerrant Word of God and the final authority on faith and practice." Those who depart from that Way are "sinners and deserve punishment in Hell."

Or take James C. Dobson of Focus on the Family, who states without a hint of nuance that "God's design for the family is rooted in biblical truth." Or take ex-pizza king Thomas Monaghan's Ave Maria Law School, whose initial mission was to turn American jurisprudence away from the Constitution and toward Roman Catholic canon law.

None of that represents the sense of seeking or truth in a strictly religious sense—if religion is the exercise of restraint. William James in *Pragmatism*[6] came closer when he wrote, "The true is the name of whatever proves itself to be good in the way of belief" and "the only test of probable truth is what works best in the way of leading us, what fits every part of life best and combines with the collectivity of experience's demands." It was the Enlightenment that changed the way humankind, at least in the West, apprehended what James called "the true." In commentary given in the 2002 William E. Massey Sr. Lectures in the History of American Civilization at Harvard University, E.L. Doctorow ob-

---

5. Founder of secular humanist Judaism and of the Birmingham Temple, Farmington Hills, Michigan, d. July 21, 2007.

6. James, *Pragmatism*, 42, 44.

served that the truth about things has been apprehended in a new way since "Bacon and Galileo insisted on putting claims of knowledge to the test with observation and experience." That approach to knowing "the true" ushered in the age of science and began what would turn out to be a never-ending effort to drive theism and theistic religion out of the department of truth-declaring and into the realm of poetry.

A great deal of Sturm und Drang complicates matters in the political and social lives of Americans in the early twenty-first century. The relentless initiative of the Religious Right and its political cohorts to inject the pseudo-science known as "creationism" or "intelligent design" into public school classrooms complicates matters for electoral politics and the governance of the schools.

I am often asked if science and religion can find some common ground. Yes, they could, but . . .

The "yes" part is that science and religion as two human enterprises already do share common ground, beginning with the same terra firma upon which human beings as scientists go about scientific research and human beings as self-consciously religious persons go about their religious observances—both being subject to the law of gravity together with the spatial and temporal limitations of having to be in one place at a time.

The "but" part has to do with how human beings as scientists arrive at their conclusions, which, if they are truly scientists, are always provisional conclusions; it has also to do with how many human beings as religious persons arrive at their conclusions, which are not always or even mostly provisional in nature. The difference is in methodology.

Scientists begin with observation of whatever phenomenon or phenomena are within their interest. They observe what anyone with the proper equipment or training may observe, all observers presumably seeing or hearing or smelling or tasting or touching or otherwise objectively discerning what is there to be observed or discerned. The shorthand term for what is being observed is "data." In the dictionary at my desk, the word "data" is defined thus: "factual information used as a basis for reasoning, discussion or calculation."[7] The key word here may be "factual." That which is factual is related to the noun "fact," which in the aforementioned dictionary is defined as "actuality, something that has actual existence, a piece of information presented as having objective reality."[8]

Thus the archaeologist at the dig comes upon a shard of unknown provenance. He or she examines it on the spot, then tries to relate it to other shards and artifacts to gather a fuller picture of what it might be and be related to. He or she does not at first exclaim, "Ah, a chip off the Holy Grail" or "A shaving off the cross of Christ." No archaeologist who would say such a thing would long be taken seriously by other archaeologists.

So the methodology of science is pretty clear. Observe, analyze, synthesize, hypothesize, test, retest to prove the hypothesis false until at some point it seems to explain the phenomenon under consideration. Charles Darwin did not set out to prove a preconceived idea that species evolve through natural selection. It may, in fact, have been the furthest thing from his mind as he strolled up the gangplank of the Beagle that December day in 1831. And only the barest beginnings of it may have been stirring as he walked back down almost five years later in October 1836. It would be twenty-two years before *The Origin of Species* would appear. Sometimes science and scientists take their good old time. I have never yet known a true scientist who wants deliberately to be caught out on a hasty mistake or conclusion.

Contrast that methodology with the general approach of self-consciously religious people, notable among whom may be theologians. They customarily bring to the creation of belief systems creedal certitudes from other ages that have somehow been certified as "orthodox" and therefore beyond both debate and discussion. Such terms as "god" are used as if they had objective referents

7. *Merriam-Webster's Collegiate Dictionary*, Tenth ed., 293.

8. Ibid., 416.

whose existence it is necessary to affirm "on faith." It is then said by some who use the term "god" that god created all things visible and invisible, seen and unseen—and that by divine fiat. Some who say such things go so far as to say that said creation was accomplished in six days—just as "it says in the Bible." Such a dictum must be accepted as objective truth because the Bible says so, and the Bible is "the word of God." This is the kind of unreason that makes people like Sam Harris and Richard Dawkins apoplectic and gives religion a bad name.

As we have observed, the term "religion" is derived from the Latin *religare,* the meaning of which goes to "restraint" or the state of being "self-restrained." There is an ethical undertone to the root word which suggests that a religious person is a person who is restrained or self-restrained from speech and action that violates another person's freedom and dignity. A religious person, for example, doesn't smite the first cheek and, in fact, if he is a religious person who subscribes to the teachings of Jesus, turns his own cheek to a would-be smiter.

On a grander scale, a religious person (by this general definition) is self-restrained from imposing his views or beliefs on another but is content with living out those beliefs, letting them speak for themselves. In an Enlightenment world, one supposes that a religious person will be self-restrained from enunciating (much less trying to insinuate in public policy) beliefs that fly in the face of known facts or well-thought-out provisional explanations about such-and-such a thing or how such-and-such a thing works and can be predicted to work again and again. In a world of good manners, one supposes that a religious person also will be self-restrained from imposing his or her beliefs upon those who do not believe at all. Alas, such is not often—or often enough—the case, out of which situation, I suppose, came the question, "Can't science and religion just find common ground?" They do, perforce, as I have pointed out. But can they in the academy and in civic life?

Several friends who are in one way or another involved in scientific research and in the teaching of one or another of the sciences often complain they are too frequently put on the defensive by representatives of religious groups asking or even requiring them to explain why scientists are so antipathetic to religion. My scientist friends say to me they don't even think about religion and its discontents as they go about their business, though a number of the scientists I know are also members of religious congregations. They cherish their religious affiliation for the ties it provides to family history and tradition, for the social outlets it provides and for the opportunities to be active and helpful in various community and outreach projects. They do not cling to their synagogues or churches because they think their religions speak the truth about, for example, how life on Earth came to be. They have other reasons for their religious affiliation, but they are not relevant to this inquiry.

It does no good to tell the religious fundamentalist his fiercely held belief that Earth was created only 6,000 years ago in pretty much the way Genesis chapter 1 tells it does not square with the facts as they are generally to be known. It does no good to tell him that his beloved Genesis seems to have been written to meet inquiries other than those concerning the origin of life. It does no good to tell him his claim to the effect that Genesis is part of a collection of documents all of which constitute "the Word of God" is an impossible conceit. He is trapped in his own argument: If the Bible (including Genesis) is the word of his god, then what it allegedly says about the origins of Earth and its species must be objectively and absolutely true. The hope for common ground fades.

What if Genesis chapter 1 through verse 2a of chapter 2 was not intended to provide any technical answers to questions of origins? How might an answer to that question be determined according to the academic method of inquiry which would at one and the same time satisfy the scientist and the scholar of biblical texts? One would first try to determine the provenance of the text.

Patient and exhaustive research has been expended on that issue for going on 200 years. So one might say there is general scholarly consensus that the passage comes from the postexilic period in Israel's history when, under Persian influence, Israel's leaders were trying to cobble together a tradition from the shards of a fairly difficult past, during part of which they had experienced what we might call indentured servitude.

So they begin to tell their story as if from the beginning of time to establish certain principles, namely: (1) the purposive force that begat the world had always had the emergence of the human creature in mind; (2) the human creature would be paramount in the order of things and, indeed, an intimate expression of the nature of that force, possessing a measure of its will and qualities; (3) the creative force was not inexhaustible, requiring respite from the creative labors; (4) in the same way the human creature being an expression, albeit a finite one, required and needed all the more such respite and, in fact, deserved it.

Read in that way, the passage seems to have more to do with, well, labor negotiations. In fact, it may be one of the first recorded sets of worker demands—to wit, for one day off in seven. Thus instead of being a treatise on the origin of life, Genesis chapter 1 and following may be an ethical argument for the treatment of human beings as if they were divine.

Now, of course, such a hypothesis is debatable and falsifiable, and such journeyman scholars as I and such master scholars as my mentors are at work on testing such hypotheses—and, in point of fact, many, many other hypotheses in the enterprise known as bible scholarship. And should one wish to group bible scholarship with religion in general, then it can be said that religion and science can share the common ground at least of methodology.

Now to suppress the bile rising in Prof. Dawkins' throat, let us agree that in no way does any part of the Jewish-Christian scriptures known as the Bible, nor of the Qur'an nor of the Upanishads or the Vedas of Hinduism, nor yet of the Sutras of Buddhism, prove that any god is real, except in the imaginations of those responsible for the authorship of those texts. What such texts tell us is that human beings for a very long time and in a great many places have imagined and even posited the existence of deities. But the texts are a matter for anthropological research to extract some workable ideas as to why it was found necessary, helpful, or desirable here and there in the human epoch to posit such deities. What do the profiles of the imagined deities tell us about their imaginers, about their times and places and situations? And in greater scope, what can we learn about Homo sapiens and his penchant for such imaginings? Such a question can certainly be asked without the Dawkins chip on the shoulder, taking seriously the pervasive phenomenon of religious experience which, as William James taught us, comes in great variety. It is not coincidental that James began serious studies as a comparative anatomist, moved from there to medicine and physiology and on to psychology and finally to philosophy and religious studies. Was James aware of Francis Bacon's dictum that it is infinitely better to begin in doubt and end, if at all possible, in certitude, than to begin in certitude and almost assuredly end in the confusion of doubts?[9] In any event, James' own variety of religious experience was thoroughly empirical and analytical in nature and, as such, not antagonistic to science.

The ancient Semites' *el*—the unseen force that was supposed to have powered and controlled phenomena, the causes of which were otherwise unknown and thought to be unknowable—eventually became coterminous with "father," king," and "master." There may have been a time in the stream of thought eventually conceptualized by Jewish-Christian thinkers when *el* played a minor to nonexistent role. What became the biblical Israel seems not to have been the consequence of a major migration of Egyptian slaves across the Sinai Peninsula or along the Red Sea or Sea of Reeds. No archaeological evidence exists to support that well-known myth. The evidence points in another direction, to a migration, all right,

---

9. Bacon, *The Advancement of Learning,* bk. 1, v. 8.

but of members of lower social classes out of the economic oligarchies of the coastal cities of the Mediterranean up into the hill
country of what is now far-northern Palestine—this occurring in
the early- to mid-thirteenth century BCE.[10] The reasons for the migration seem to have been what usually causes human migrations:
starvation, oppression, violence, and a desire for a new and better
life. The coastal cities apparently had a very hierarchical economic
system with a very few controlling very much of what resources
existed with little to no significant trickle down—not entirely unlike the economic situation being spurred on in this country now
with the fabulous tax cuts for the super-rich at the expense of the
poor, just to offer a helpful analogy.

Those not in the kind embrace of the oligarchies had two
choices: mass revolt, in which they would probably have been cru-
elly subjugated, or emigration. They chose the latter. Archaeologists
have found, they think, ancient remains of those migrant communities in the hardscrabble hill country east of the Mediterranean.
The archaeological finds suggest that those communities had no
military, that they were egalitarian in nature and governed themselves with what we might call today "ethical covenants" formed
or crafted on an "If A, then B" basis. As in, "If you knowingly steal
your neighbor's cow, you must return it promptly with the equiva-
lence of whatever benefit you may have derived from having it in
your possession." It's called case law—the record of communities
trying to find their way to successful self-governance in peaceful
and nonviolent ways, far from the opposites with which they previously lived.

What the record suggests as we find it in the Bible is that the
inevitable occurred. Since the word "utopia" means "no place," and
since those communities were actual people in actual places, that
almost utopian life could not and would not last forever. There is
always the will to power, and the growing complexity of life. Soon
enough the deceptively simple case laws of the egalitarian com-

10. Meyers, *Exodus,* 165, 179.

munities got systematized into codes for the sake of more permanence and dependability—for much the same reasons, I suppose, the United States Constitution eventually succeeded the Articles of Confederation, which itself was a successor to various local jurisprudential customs. But back to the thirteenth century BCE.

Imagine how the codification of those communal case laws may have occurred. We all know the story of Mount Sinai and Cecil B. DeMille's gigantic hand extending the tablets of the law to Charlton Heston. For the convenience of the children of Israel, Yahweh had chiseled the first of what would become 613 mitzvoth on the stone. It surprises me to know how many people still believe more or less that's how it happened: *fiat lex*—in the same way that creation began *fiat lux*. If we understand that the fiat of creation is a dynamic process still in progress as Darwin and Einstein have helped us understand it, then we can readily understand the evolution of law. Imagine the tribal elders gathered around the fire at night trying to figure out how to keep their newly founded communities in one piece. Previously they had been subjected to the legal whims of their oppressors. Now they were on their own, trying to settle things case by case. One wise old elder observes that if only the community could somehow proscribe envy, they could curb stealing. Then another observes that if stealing could be made less socially acceptable by increasing community disapproval, maybe people would be less likely to turn to violence and killing to obtain what they envied. Adultery, being envy acted out in an unmistakable way, had a similar deleterious effect, so it, too, was proscribed. Eventually, as the elders began to die off, it became necessary to establish some kind of posthumous authority for their wisdom. Hence the mandate to "honor thy father and mother."

Communities increase in number—if they can manage to survive famine and prolonged warfare—and thereby become more complex. Just as the United States of America, even in its inception, could not suffer itself to be governed by the New England town meeting formula but had to resort to representative democracy, so the members of those communities of antiquity ceded authority to appointed (or often enough, self-appointed) leaders who, as human nature would have it, sought aggrandizement as privilege. Soon enough those leaders morphed into priests and kings, the former to speak for the deities they invented to support their position, the latter to enforce the control their invented god or gods allegedly gave them. One can see how all that got out of hand, and one can read several versions of how it did in the biblical books of Samuel and King. Into that morass of the corruption of power stepped the public intellectuals we call the prophets with their calls for reform, justice, and nonviolence. Their sixth-century BCE successors became heralds of and advocates for postexilic restoration with the same underlying themes of social and economic justice.

It was that not-always constant stream of thought that Hillel the Elder and his near-contemporaries John the Baptist and Jesus of Nazareth are depicted as having articulated. The Baptist's message as recalled by Luke was "bear fruits worthy of repentance [that is, of a change of mind and heart] . . . whoever has two coats must share with anyone who has none; and whoever has food must do likewise."[11] There is a clue to the economic situation for Judeans in the first third of the first century CE. The implication of the Baptist's exhortation is that there were people without clothing and without food. Therefore, the response was no complicated belief system, no ornate ritual, but rather meeting human need with requisite resources—a prophetic call, indeed.

But even as that version of the Baptist's preaching ministry was being spun out, Luke was being overtaken by the mythmaking that began with Paul some forty years earlier as quite quickly the convert apostle seized upon the small movement that probably grew up around the ethical sayings of Jesus—one of a number of itinerant sages.[12]

---

11. Luke 3:10.

12. A term coined by Crossan; see esp. *Jesus: A Revolutionary Biography,* 102–22.

Perhaps Paul could see that the passage of time and events would eclipse the significance of Jesus' message if the message were not provided with a vehicle to move it along through history. So Paul recast the Sage of Nazareth as a universal cosmic figure. Here is how Paul (or some Paul-like imitator) put it in the epistle to the churches of Colossae: "He [Christ] is the image of the invisible God, the firstborn of all creation, for in him all things in heaven and earth were created . . . he himself is before all things, and in him all things hold together."[13] Written, say, twenty-five years after the Jesus of the gospels would have lived, this sentiment would, I am sure, have shocked Jesus as he was washing the grit of Palestine trails off his gnarled feet on the way from where he'd been to where he was headed.

Or take this line, obviously quoted with great relish by Paul in his Philippian epistle drawing from some earlier source: "Christ Jesus . . . was in the form of God but did not regard equality with God as something to be exploited," the passage ending with the paean "at the name of Jesus every knee should bend in heaven and on earth and under the earth, and every tongue confess that Jesus Christ is Lord, to the glory of God the Father.[14]

Even Luke, the great universalist-humanist, slips into that stream with his depiction in the Acts of the Apostles of the recently rehabilitated Christ-denier, Peter, informing his fellow Jews, "There is salvation in no one else, for there is no other name under heaven given among mortals by which we must be saved."[15] Add all that to the first 18 verses of John's gospel, which equate Christ with the eternal wisdom and heart of God, and you have laid the groundwork for an imperial religion. Now nearly fully formed, Christianity, which began its life as an ethical movement I call "Jesus Judaism," actually became imperialistic but as yet with no empire.

13. Colossians 1:15–17.
14. Philippians 2:5–11.
15. Acts 4:12.

Irenaeus, the second-century bishop of Lugundum in Gaul—better known today as Lyon in France—was instrumental in establishing the constructs of Paul and John as normative Christian philosophy, as Elaine Pagels so adroitly points out in her 2003 book *Beyond Belief*. Pagels hypothesizes that the Gospel of John was in part written to oppose the image of Jesus conveyed in the Gospel of Thomas—that image being of a very earthy, earthly, earth-bound Jesus who was anything but an incarnated god. Irenaeus bought totally into the Pauline and Johannine models and so delivered up Christianity ready to be co-opted by empire.

About 125 years after Irenaeus' death, Christianity, then institutionalized as the Catholic Church and still subject to persecution from time to time, was seized upon by Constantine the Great as the means to bring some kind of conformity and uniformity to the far-flung empire of which he became emperor, the last one standing of the rivals who had coveted the job. In 311 or 312, Constantine issued an edict of toleration under which Christians and their church were no longer to be persecuted or interfered with. Then, as the record suggests, he went about trying to co-opt the connectional system of the church to save his imperial bacon.

No sooner did he engineer his colorful conversion to the faith than he discovered it was riven by a number of related conflicts, some territorial power struggles and others related to what we would call today "theological disputes." Some thinkers in the early fourth century had evidently become disenchanted with Irenaeus's orthodox formula, thinking that the proclamation of Christ as God himself was a bit much. One of these thinkers was a priest named Arius who thought simple reason demanded that the church stop referring to Jesus Christ as pre-existent, as coequal and coterminous with God, and, rather, acknowledge that he was created by God just as other creatures were created. The outcry was understandable. It's hard to shore up an empire based on a creature when you could have it be based on the creator.

That was the controversy that was preoccupying the church as Constantine came shakily to power. The institution he was counting on to be a vehicle of unity and therefore of control was involved in a kind of civil war.

So he called what would become known as the First Ecumenical Council to which many, but by far not all, of the bishops of the church came. Their task? To determine once and for all the nature of Christ. It's laughable at this remove that anyone at anytime thought such truth could be arrived at by a committee of the whole. But arrive it did, after considerable time with the forces of what we would now call "orthodoxy" winning the day against Arius and his followers, who were anathematized as "heretics"— the word meaning "choosers," as in having chosen to believe other than what the controlling majority decreed.

And so it was that in due course—only seventy years before the final collapse of the Western Empire—the church became coterminous with empire and had an imperial theology to match, enabling it to institute and maintain control over great masses of people because it was perceived as having a monopoly on truth.

I think, but I cannot prove, that all Constantine wanted from the church was a little glue to hold his fractious empire together. What resulted, though, was an imperial church that would go on a millennium later to conduct the Crusades, that would torture and kill alleged heretics, that would hector reformers, that would hound the likes of Galileo to his grave, that would re-emerge in Protestant form as biblical fundamentalism, that would give the world such ecclesiastical despots as the Medicis and Pope Pius IX, and pave the way for the more uncompromising reigns of John Paul II and Benedict XVI.

4

An Agnostic Secular Humanist Works with Biblical Texts

FOR SOME it is an impossibility that the likes of me should have been admitted to the journeyman craft of biblical interpretation. I have consistently refused to affirm creeds ancient or modern and have pursued the odd science of translation and analysis of biblical texts as any archaeologist worthy of the name will examine the shards from a dig, i.e., with no preconceived notion of what they all may add up to in the end.

That I should have been thus engaged for most of the past half century as an ordained minister of the Episcopal Church has been to my critics a bitter wonderment and to my supporters a freshet of the peace that passeth understanding. Some would say there is insufficient oil in the nether regions to fry me as mercilessly as I deserve. Others have showered me with gratitude for the labor of intellectual honesty.

Withal, I have never found it necessary or desirable to attempt to force the square peg of any biblical text into the round hole of a creedal formula. In fact, I have, mostly to the purposeful discomfiture of the orthodox, done the opposite. To say that most terms of most systematic theologies are contortionist and self-serving misapplications of biblical texts is to state an obvious truth.

That a great many biblical texts are themselves the issue of theological agenda is likewise obvious, requiring interpreters to discover and account for such agenda in the pursuit of understanding the meaning of a particular chapter or verse.

One of my working hypotheses is that the New Testament documents, one and all, belong to the category of political and religious history, and in particular church history. Setting aside the unhelpful and entirely unsupportable assertion that biblical literature is exempt from the ordinary rigors of objective investigation because it is "of God," I have applied to my textual analysis the canons of academic research, going where the data lead rather than marshaling the data to lead me where a religious tradition and its hierarchy would have me led.

That said, I have relished my decades of research and analysis of the Bible's contents because I consider the Bible to be a collection of some of the most remarkable literature of antiquity. I have never experienced difficulties in building lectures, seminar outlines or sermons on biblical texts. I have not treated them as "thus-saith-the-Lord" proclamations but as attempts—some of them wondrously and profoundly creative—to account for how and why human beings have done what they have done, said what they have said and endured what they have endured.

For some time I have published online weekly exegetical essays on the readings appointed for Sunday use in the Revised Common Lectionary. The essays are read and used by clergy and lay teachers all over the United States and Canada, as well as Australia and New Zealand. Several samples of those essays follow as examples of how an agnostic secular humanist can work with biblical texts in a way that illuminates them for use in congregational life.

A READING FOR THE FIRST SUNDAY
AFTER THE EPIPHANY—YEAR C

Luke 3:15–17, 21–22

Imagine being an intelligent extraterrestrial dropping into a Christian church during the rite of baptism and wondering what the man or woman in the long white robe meant to be doing to a baby by pouring water over its head. You would probably conclude you were witnessing an antique ritual intended to wash away the evil spirits or some such thing. In a way, you would be right. Being of superior intelligence, you would know that an ounce or two of tepid water would not avail for any true cleansing. You would know further that the infant being so washed would experience probable discomfort. You would wonder at the furtive snapping of cameras and the oohing and aahing of grown-up people witnessing the event.

Depending on what kind of church you were visiting, the answer to your questions, "What's going on here and why?" could range from: "A death unto sin, and a new birth unto righteousness: for being by nature born in sin, and the children of wrath, we are hereby made the children of grace."[1] Or: "Infants are baptized so that they can share citizenship in the Covenant, membership in Christ, and redemption by God."[2] Or: "Baptism is a Sacrament which cleanses us from original sin, makes us Christians, children of God, and heirs of heaven. Actual sins and all the punishment due to them are remitted by Baptism, if the person baptized be guilty of any. Baptism is necessary to salvation, because without it we cannot enter into the kingdom of heaven."[3] Or: "Baptism is a sacrament, wherein the washing with water in the name of the Father, and of the Son, and of the Holy Ghost doth signify and seal our engrafting into Christ, and partaking of the benefits of the covenant of grace, and our engagement to be the Lord's."[4] Or: "Baptism is the first and chief sacrament of forgiveness of sins, because it unites us with Christ, who died for our sins and rose for our justification . . ."[5]

1. "A Catechism," Book of Common Prayer 1928, 581.

2. "An Outline of the Faith Commonly Called the Catechism," Book of Common Prayer 1979, 858.

3. "Lesson Fourteen: On Baptism," Questions 152–154, The Baltimore Catechism, 38.

4. "Westminster Shorter Catechism," Question 94.

5. "Catechism of the Catholic Church" 1992, # 977, On Baptism for the Forgiveness of Sins.

Now, O curious alien, what do you know?

You know as much as most, if not all, of the humans gathered at that thing called a font. Stick around and learn a thing or two about whence the strange rite you and they are witnessing.

We return to John the Baptist just as Luke gets around to the persistent first-century notion that the Baptist might have been "the One who was to come." Certainly this reflects a real situation as, perhaps, some significant number of mid- to late-first-century Jews and Gentiles were assessing the careers of the late John and the late Jesus as to which of the movements they should give loyalty. Luke makes John demur (v. 16) and actually debase himself ("I am not worthy to untie the thong of his sandals.") Then in less than typical Lucan sentiment, John is made to add all the business about the wheat and the chaff (v. 17) and the unmistakable hint of harsh judgment for those neither astute nor fortunate enough to be adjudged wheat.

Water baptism (v. 16) seems to be played down with John's "I baptize you with water, but . . ." The real baptism will be "with the Holy Spirit and with fire"—fire being a symbol of judgment and purification. See Mal 3:2b–3: "For he is like a refiner's fire . . . and he will purify the descendants of Levi and refine them . . . until they present offerings to the Lord in righteousness." Luke will later in "the second book" take the symbol of baptism by fire to new heights in the depiction of baptism/ordination of the apostles at Pentecost, which is obliquely referred to in the portion from the Acts of the Apostles (8:14–17) appointed as the second reading in this proper. See also Isa 43:2, part of this proper's first appointed reading, and its allusion to both "fire" and "water."

As to the baptism of Jesus (the liturgical theme of Epiphany I), it has been a theological puzzlement for a long time to those who wish to perpetuate the myth of Jesus' sinlessness—as if he had not been a human being with all the physical and psychic apparatus of so being. John's baptism was (or was depicted as being) for the forgiveness of sin. All four canonical gospels agree Jesus was baptized. Mark's entry: "In those days Jesus came from Nazareth of Galilee and was baptized by John in the Jordan." One would have to assume it was hearsay evidence inasmuch as the supposed event being referenced would have occurred no fewer than forty years before Mark (the gospel) was composed.

Matthew (in 3:13–17) has Jesus coming from Nazareth for the purpose of being baptized, but with an argument from John about who should baptize whom. Matthew's Jesus prevails, saying, in effect, "this will be a good example for others to follow." The Gospel of John suggests (1:31) that the Baptist came baptizing "that he (messiah/Jesus) might be revealed to Israel." John (the evangelist) finesses direct mention of Jesus' baptism at the hands of the Baptist, who is depicted as saying he didn't even know Jesus by sight, but allows him to witness to his own vision of the heavenly epiphany (1:32–34).

Sometimes Jesus' baptism is referred to by theologians as an "embarrassment," in that, by common consent of four otherwise competing gospel traditions, Jesus was for a time subordinate to John, and, furthermore, considered himself needful of a baptism (washing) meant to remove the mark of sin. That the event is nevertheless included or referred to in one way or another by all four canonical evangelists tells a great many scholars that it must actually have occurred. But why should it have not occurred? John the Baptist seems to have been as prominent, if not more so, than Jesus for a time. It may well be that Jesus or a Jesus-type was drawn to the charismatic figure of the Baptist and later broke with him ideologically or succeeded him after the Baptist's imprisonment and eventual execution.[6]

J. D. Crossan has made a point now and again of contrasting the Baptist's evident apocalyptic nature with Jesus' sapiential approach—not so much that the coming of the kingdom is in sight with all its portent but that the kingdom is within. The Baptist is generally depicted as renouncing the world. Jesus is depicted as

---

6. Josephus, *Antiquities of the Jews,* Book 18, Ch. 5, 2.

embracing the world and guiding people in the development of an ethic to make it a world that could work.

Assuming that a Jesus was among those baptized by John for forgiveness, perhaps it may be said that Jesus (or those writing about him) may have evolved a different meaning of baptism than John or anyone else had intended. Maybe as the image of Jesus matured in the development of the gospels, it came to be seen that forgiveness of sin had less to do with preparation for the end of something than with a new beginning.

Whatever else the rite of baptism is, it does draw a line in time between something before and something after. The question in both directions is "What?" The catechisms quoted above say baptism effects a change in and for the baptized from a former state of exclusion to a new one of inclusion—inclusion in a kingdom or a covenant, whatever. A theologian would say it was an "ontological" matter or one of "being." Before baptism the person in question "was" something. Now he/she "is" something different.

This is where our E.T. friend would have to shake his head in wonderment. He could easily see that the infant over whom the water of baptism was poured was the same bedewed as unbedewed. If Mr. E.T. were to voice that thought, the priest or minister at the font might tell him that what he saw was "an outward and visible sign of an inward and spiritual grace." The stranger might wish to phone home for an explanation.

E.T. would probably realize that the infant in question would have no memory of the occasion. The assumption might be that those things promised by the adults who had been gathered around the font would, if delivered on, help produce the ontological state envisioned by the rite.

What if E.T. had dropped into an Episcopal church that used the 1979 rite and heard these words:

(Question to the sponsors or to an adult candidate) *"Will you strive for justice and peace among all people, and respect the dignity of every human being?"*

(Answer of sponsors or of adult candidate) *"I will, with God's help."*[7]

In that case E.T. would understand that the strange rite he had witnessed was pointed outward to the world and had to do not with an ontological value but an ethical one. The vow asked and given was to engage the world at the points where justice needed to be done and peace needed to be made beginning with respecting the dignity of every person.

Now, E.T. would say to himself, "I see the point of it all." He would say, "It's all on those adults who gave the vows for the infant. If they do their job and raise the kid on peace and justice values and human dignity, all this was worth it."

A READING FOR THE FOURTH SUNDAY AFTER THE EPIPHANY—YEAR C

Luke 4:1–13

"Months in due succession, days of lengthening light."[8] Even though that text appears in a hymn associated with Easter, it is a reference to the season that, with Ash Wednesday, has just commenced. "Lent" is a derivation of "lengthening" from the Old English *lencten*.

Lent's theological denouement is Passiontide and Easter with all the mythology that has overlaid the Jesus movement almost from its beginnings. Since there is no end to commentary written with orthodox believers and practitioners in mind, our task for the next six editions of this series will be to make biblical texts accessible to unbelievers, atheists, agnostics, and secular humanists.

Luke was, of course, dependent on Mark and then Matthew for the narrative known as "the temptation of Jesus in the wilderness." Either that or the text was so well-known that each evange-

---

7. "The Baptismal Covenant," Book of Common Prayer 1979, 306.

8. Fortunatus, "Welcome, Happy Morning."

list was in singular receipt of it. Mark's version is typically brief and spare (Mark 1:12–13) with none of the drama Matthew provides (4:1–11) and which Luke altered some. Missing from Matthew and Luke are Mark's characteristic "immediately" (*euthus*) and "the wild beasts." Matthew and Luke add three particular "temptations" (from the Greek verb *peirazō*, "to test or prove").

The tester for Matthew and Luke is the devil (*diabolos*) and for Mark, satan. *Diabolos* literally means "one who throws [*balos*] something across [*dia*, as in diagonally] one's path." "Satan" is a stab at spelling or pronouncing a Semitic root *stn*, which suggests an adversarial role.[9]

Matthew and Luke chose diabolos as the name of the tester or agency of the testing, suggesting perhaps that the opportunities for self-aggrandizement (stones into bread), exploitation of power (throwing oneself down from a pinnacle) and, for a price, the acquisition of temporal power (the worship of power itself) were stumbling blocks thrown across Jesus' path to deter him. And while we will be rationalizing those images, no doubt the evangelists took for granted the presence of cunning and malign powers to which they did not hesitate to impute personal characteristics.

Luke's order of the testing is different from Matthew's. Matthew has the stones into bread first, then flinging from the Temple pinnacle and the vision of power from the mountain. Luke puts the vision of power first and the pinnacle scene second. Luke actually omits mention of a mountain, merely saying *diabolos* "took Jesus up," i.e., turned his horizontal path into a vertical one. Did Luke omit "mountain" because his use of the word in 9:28 connotes a place of quiet contemplation, or because it was silly to suggest that no spot however high could be high enough for the human eye to see the whole of things, "all the kingdoms of the world"?

Matthew uses the broader term *kosmos* for world while Luke uses *oikumenā*, meaning "the inhabited earth," or where people live.

---

9. Pagels, *The Origin of Satan*, 39.

When one considers the many more and well-known testings to which flesh is subject, one wonders why the evangelists do not mention an obvious one: sexual temptation. Maybe because even to mention it would have threatened their nascent Christology.

Jesus' responses to his testings are all scriptural: "One does not live by bread alone" (Deut 8:3), "Worship the Lord your God and serve him only" (Deut 6:13), and "Do not put the Lord your God to the test" (Deut 6:16). This latter quotation says, in effect, that human beings are subjected to testing or proving, but should not in turn attempt to subject the biblical deity. The Gospel of John includes no such testing or proving narrative in keeping with the Christology of its prologue (1:1–18) which proclaims that the one who was "was in the beginning with God," while human, was never not divine.

In both Matthew and Luke, *diabolos* quotes scripture back to Jesus (Pss 91:11–12): "He will command his angels concerning you. . . . On their hands they will bear you up, so that you will not dash your foot against a stone." Such a characterization of *diabolos* suggests that in both evangelists' minds the diabolic power was intimately knowledgeable and quite possibly an inner voice representing a darker side of human nature.

Though classic Hebraism was not dualistic, by the late first century CE the whole area known to the authors and editors of Matthew and Luke was fully hellenized and therefore acquainted with Platonic dualism. If Luke did not go so far as to locate in Jesus an evil that was diametrically opposed to good, he certainly at the least saw Jesus as good arrayed against diabolos as evil—evil in the sense that diabolos was imagined as behaving true to form, i.e., deterring, detouring, and confusing.

Mark and Matthew end the testing narrative by saying that angels (delegated messengers) ministered to Jesus. Luke merely hits the pause button, saying that diabolos, having finished the current mission (literally, "completed every test"), put distance between himself and Jesus "until an opportune time."

Luke uses "diabolos" four times in the narrative at hand and once more at 8:12 and then switches to "satan" for five entries (10:18, 11:18, 13:16, 22:3) and two more in Acts (5:3 and 26:18).

Jesus, foretold in Luke 1, born in 2, baptized in 3, and tested in 4, is now ready to begin his public career, which he does among his hometown folk in their Nazarene synagogue—stories we have heard earlier in this Year C, thanks to the trajectory of the RCL.

No matter how much mythology there is in the gospels, no matter the unnecessarily complex creedal formulae laid down by centuries of theologians like so many busy bees in a hive, the personage or character we refer to as "Jesus" was human. He was a man. He could have been a woman, but all sources say he was a man. Either way, as a human being he would have been and surely was subject to all that makes one human, which is to say vulnerable.

Human beings by nature are vulnerable—vulnerable to exertions of pride and prejudice, to overreaching, to fits of anger, to being irrational at exactly the moments quiet reason would be most desirable.

Indeed, human beings are wont to see pearls of what they think are of great price and just as wont to climb over anything and anyone in their headlong rush to obtain them. Sometimes those pearls are fake and of very little price, sometimes things not good for those who pursue them.

That's a good time for what Luke calls "the devil" to throw that cross-body block (*dia-bolos*) on the pursuer and make him stop. And if he is stopped for long enough, he may have thrust upon him that all-important moment in which to ask, "Why am I doing this?"

The diabolos may not be a dead stop but a detour. Maybe what one seeks is a fine thing, but the way he goes about obtaining it is not a good way. Then the path is diverted to a better, maybe safer, way.

The great human "sin"—if sin is a word we must use—may be not thinking before we act, or not thinking hard enough, or not counting the cost, and figuring out if the promise is worth the cost.

If the gospels are taken at face value, they portray the adult Jesus in the last year or two or three of his life (depending on which gospel account is credited) embarked on a path, the end of which could only be just about what he got out of it: arrest, trial, conviction, and execution.

Maybe the classic temptation-of-Jesus-in-the-wilderness story heard every year on the First Sunday in Lent was an interior experience. Maybe Jesus made a retreat all by himself, and went out among the owls and scorpions to ask if it was hunger for recognition he sought ("Make this stone into a loaf of bread"), to ask if it was power he sought ("See these great kingdoms? Give all your energies and loyalty to power, and you can have them"), and to ask himself if he really wanted to prove his prowess in a carnival-like fashion ("Throw yourself off the pinnacle of the Temple and hope for the best").

The answers he is depicted as coming up with were the product of rather tortured but rational consideration. That which was thrown across his path did not, in the end, keep him from taking it. What was thrown across his path helped him understand what the cost of taking it would be. He would say what he had to say and do what he had to do on the way down the path he set before himself, as best as he could predict its route and its end point.

A READING FOR THE FIFTH SUNDAY
AFTER THE EPIPHANY

Luke 5:1–11

The readings appointed in the RCL for Epiphany V-C have to do thematically with vocation—not deciding to do something but to be called to do it. It is hard to argue with someone who says he or she was "called" to a task or a profession. George W. Bush once said he believed "God" called him to be president of the United States. I remember an Episcopal bishop once telling several hundred of his flock that "God called me to be your bishop." The looks of astonishment exchanged by several present featured wide eyes and raised brows. One skeptic was heard to whisper rhetorically, "What god?"

You can't beat the first Isaiah's "call" as related in the first reading of this proper: Isa 6:1–8. It is the eighth-century BCE prophet's account of a visionary experience in the course of which he believed Yahweh had indirectly summoned him by asking, "Whom shall I send and who will go for us?" (perhaps also in the rhetorical vein). With the bizarre vision of seraphim flying hither and thither through his imagination, Isaiah hears himself saying, "I'm here. Send me."

What he saw and heard became his impetus for volunteering—not an unreasonable basis for making a life-changing decision. The founder of an inner-city social service agency in which I now volunteer was going about the proper sacramental business of being a priest until he met a man called "Dave" who, out of his poverty and loss, showed the priest what he needed to do with his priesthood.

Out of that real-life vision the priest founded the agency "where cross the crowded ways of life" to which those "in haunts of wretchedness and need, on shadowed thresholds dark with fears"[10] now come day in and day out, week in and week out, year in and year out, for succor.

Now the other call/calling.

It is time in the Lucan scheme of things to put names and intentions on Jesus' followers. Luke's Jesus has already in this gospel attracted considerable attention, not all of it positive (4:29). Now Luke will have him call fishers of fish to become "fishers of people" (5:10). Mark started the "fishermen" story (1:16ff). Matthew continued it in 4:18ff. It is left to Luke, however, to embellish the story in good Lucan style with great shoals of fish, nets breaking under the load, boats shipping water.

You wonder if Luke and John used a common story (see John 21:4–11). There is only one boat in John, though two in Luke's version. Not to put too fine a point on it, John even gives the number of the fish: 153. In dealing with this text, one does well to remember that fish and fishing were important to Palestinians of the day. Fish was a major dietary staple for those who could get it. Luke was attentive to the local color when aware of it.

The gospel passage at hand has Jesus suddenly going from Judea (4:44) to the shores of the lake of Gennesaret, also known as the Sea of Galilee and about fifteen miles at its nearest point from Nazareth. Luke depicts Jesus standing on the shore just as John Wesley went to the coal mines —where the working people were in the midst of commerce. No out-of-touch religion here.

Three of those who will turn out to be disciples are named in Luke 5. The first is thrice called "Simon" (verses 3–5) then "Simon Peter" (verse 8) and back to "Simon" (verses 9–10). The others are the brothers Zebedee, James and John, who, it is said, were partners in the fishing business with Simon/Peter. This gives Jesus three close followers with others yet to come.

---

10. North, "Where Cross the Crowded Ways of Life," #609 in The Hymnal 1982.

Like the first Isaiah's vision, the scene at the lake was an occurrence that Simon/Peter and the Zebedees are depicted as finding extraordinary.

But we must go back a moment or two in time to the initial encounter. Jesus appears at the lake, observing the fishermen cleaning out their fish-less boats after a night of trolling. Luke's story is suspenseful. Jesus is made to get into one of the boats and give advice, bidding them put out a bit from land and let down the nets they had just brought in to dry. Like all fishermen, they are made to roll their eyes at such amateurish counsel, yet, again like all fishermen, they hold out hope for a catch of any kind, and so, after some argument, yield. The upshot is said to have been a catch beyond belief.

In Luke's imagination, that did it for Peter, who is made to kneel and bid Jesus go away from him "for I am a sinful one," meaning that Peter, sensing he was in the presence of serious power and purpose, decided it was no time to be anything but utterly reverent. Luke winds up the story by saying of Peter, James and John that, after they brought their boats to shore, "they left everything and followed him."

Isaiah was depicted as offering himself to be sent. Peter & Co. were depicted as being dazzled and following one they believed represented power. It is not recorded whether or not the first Isaiah flagged in zeal. It is most certainly recorded that those who are said to have followed Jesus did exactly that. All four canonical evangelists are careful to depict the future holder of the keys of the kingdom saying "I do not know the man" when accused of being associated with Jesus after his arrest. So much for the catch of fish back there on Gennesaret's shore. (See Mark 14:66–72; Matt 26:69–75; Luke 22:55–62 and John 18:25–27.)

For more excitement, see the epistle reading for this proper (1 Cor 15:1–11) which may be the real story of Paul's "conversion."

It is said that Isaiah saw the hem of Yahweh's robe fill the temple, Peter and his partners with an unprecedented catch of fish, and Paul a dead man living.

My late friend, Father James McLaren, saw Dave battered and beaten down by the government agencies that were meant to help him but stole his dignity instead. Seeing that moved (or called, if you must) Father McLaren to start his own agency, which to this day emphasizes the dignity of every man, woman, and child who comes to its door.

One homiletic key to unlocking the twenty-first-century meaning for these readings is a reprise of meaning for these readings is a reprise of playwright Arthur Miller's unforgettable line in "Death of a Salesman": "Attention must be paid."

It's not so difficult for previously unsuccessful fishermen to pay attention to nets full of fish suddenly appearing. It's not that much more difficult to pay attention to the story of a eighth-century BCE public intellectual being caught up in a vision of seraphim. One hesitates to pay undue attention to a story of an otherwise sane and intelligent man who says he encountered a living one thought dead.

What's really difficult is being able to see in "Dave," as Father McLaren saw him, a human summons to go a different way. No one but Willy Loman's own wife saw him as one to whom attention should be paid. "He's a human being, and a terrible thing is happening to him. So attention must be paid. He's not to be allowed to fall into his grave like an old dog," she said of her husband.

Attention was paid by Father McLaren, and what he saw of Dave's situation moved him to help restore and maintain Dave's dignity and, through the agency founded on the basis of that experience, the dignity of almost 100,000 other Daves since.

If it's a lesson in discipleship you're seeking, there it is.

READINGS FOR THE FOURTH SUNDAY IN LENT—
YEAR C

Joshua 5:9–12, 2 Cor 5:16–21, Luke 15:11–32

You have to search for it in the Joshua and Corinthian readings, but it is writ large in the gospel lection. The concept is "redemption," as in the mainly Hebrew idea of negotiating the return of an alienated property or treasure that was taken by force or sold in trade, or had merely separated itself and become lost.

In the Joshua reading, the Israelites' fictive emancipation[11] from Egypt is recalled as they dine no longer on manna[12] but on the produce of the land in which they find themselves free at last and which they shall eventually occupy. The effect of whatever supposedly took them into Egypt had been neutralized, and they now stood "redeemed"—in effect, bought or brought back into the embrace of the deity of their fathers.

In 2 Corinthians 5, one of the denser passages of Paul's theology, it is said that Paul's deity—probably in his imagination an amalgam of Zeus, Yahweh, and the Logos—basically determined to re-create the creation and, in the process, reconcile the old one to himself through the ministration of the divine self as represented in the one Paul calls "Christ," or the anointed one. Reconciliation is part of the action of redemption.

---

11. There exists no archaeological evidence for the Exodus as it is depicted in the Bible. The more probable explanation for the tribal presence in Canaan of those who became Jews is that they migrated from eastern coastal cities of the Mediterranean, which were economic oligarchies, into the hill country of what is now northern Israel, where they settled in simple, egalitarian communities.

12. Manna, from the Hebrew *man-hu* ("what is it?") is a natural honeylike substance excreted by desert insects, but depicted in the Bible as a gift sent down by Yahweh to assuage the Israelites' hunger in their transit from Egypt to the promised land.

That set of ideas is seen more clearly in the passage known as the parable of the prodigal son, being perhaps the most excellent grace note in the whole of the New Testament. It certainly ranks in the Christian world with the Twenty-third Psalm, 1 Corinthians 13 and the Lord's Prayer for cherished religious texts. One wants very much to think that someone named Jesus—"the" Jesus to more orthodox believers—told this story pretty much as it appears in Luke 15. If "a" or "the" Jesus did not tell the story or one very much like it, the parable's sentiment nonetheless fits well with the ethic of one of the prominent sayings attributed to a Jesus: "Forgive seventy times seven" (Matt 18:21, var. Luke 17:4).

To believe with any intellectual honesty that "the" Jesus told the prodigal's story, one would have to posit an early and original source for it, which some analysts have done (calling it "L"), and which only Luke would have known about and/or which only Luke used. If it were not original with Luke or some proto-Lucan tradition, surely any gospel writer would have included it in some form. Yet the story appears only in Luke.

Of course, neither the prodigal son story nor its theme of unconditional forgiveness fits too well with Matt 25:31–46, wherein judgment, not forgiveness, is paramount. Also it is not likely that much first-century CE Jesus Judaism, not to mention emerging synagogue Judaism, would have been ready for the universalism generally expressed by Luke in the parable.

A good many exegetes have turned themselves into eisegetes in their efforts to parse this parable, e.g., treating it as an allegory. Called "the parable of the prodigal son" by translators of the English bible of the late 1500s, its central figure is certainly the father. And while the dispositions and actions of both younger and elder sons are the color and melodrama of the piece, it is the father's disposition and action that make the story what it is and that gives the parabolic point to it—the point being that the father's love for both his sons extends to understanding and forgiving their rejections: of him by the younger, and of the younger by the elder.

One can make a case that the original parable (whether from the lips of "a" or "the" Jesus) comprises verses 1–24 while 25–32 constitute a kind of midrash added later. There is much to commend such a hypothesis inasmuch as 15:24 reads like a dramatic ending: " 'This son of mine was dead and is alive; he was lost and is found!' And they began to celebrate," which is the father's uncompromising explanation for the feast.

If, as I have long proposed, the gospels are in large part the history of nascent Christianity, verses 25–32 may have been added to take into account the rift between the more or less established communities of Jesus Judaism and Gentile converts—the figure of the elder son being a sympathetic contact point for Jews who may have felt ill-used by the ready acceptance of uninitiated Gentile converts. Think here of the conflict depicted in Acts 15:1–29 and Gal 2:1–21 and of the meditative role assigned by Luke to James in Acts 15:13–21.

Rudolf Bultmann and others insist that that Luke 15:11–32 is of a piece and in more or less its original form (whatever they mean by "original"), and that the two distinct sections of the parable are necessary to the main point of the whole, viz. that divine forgiveness embraces both the egregious and blasphemous wastrel and the faithful but intolerant good brother.

VERSE NOTES

Verse 12: Luke has the younger son ask for his patrimony as if his father was already dead. Since he was chronologically the second of two sons, the older would, by custom of the time and place, get two-thirds of the estate and he himself one-third. Luke says the father "divided" the substance between them, meaning perhaps that Luke for theological purposes wanted to depict the abused father as being even more generous than custom provided. In any event, it appears that in Luke's imagination the father held on to much of his wealth, through the process of what we would call today life estate, to continue the home-front enterprise and to be able (and ready, as it turns out) to lay on a big feast upon the prodigal's return.

Verse 13 says the younger son "gathered all he had." The Greek term here is *sunagōgā* from the verb *sunagein*, meaning, in this case, converting material property to cash, making the inheritance portable.

Verse 17: "When he came to himself"—i.e., when sobriety and common sense returned—in Luke's imagination he began to calculate the cost of his stupidity and resultant loss, and composed a speech to give to his father on whose mercy he was about to throw himself. He can't even get to the front door before his father meets him on the road and leads him back into the bosom of his family. The point is that he was *nekros* (dead) and now, the joyous father proclaims, is alive. The death may refer to the custom of the time to the effect that a son who treated a father as the prodigal had was as good as dead, cut off not by the family but by the exercise of his own poor choice.

Verse 25 depicts the elder son busy at his appointed work, even though Luke depicts him as in possession of his two-thirds of the estate, in which, as we have observed, his father held life estate. The father attempts to explain to the elder son why the hoopla for the younger. No record is made of how it went for the younger son after the party or whether the two sons ever reconciled.

That's a parable for you. You identify with its oft-told story and perhaps with one character or another, maybe not the same one each time. Thus the story ends up meaning one thing to one person and another to the next, and to each a different thing at a different time.

My revered teacher, the late Dr. George A. Buttrick, said of this parable: "No story more instantly touches the nerve of actual life. Let it be read, without any comment or explanation, and it conquers us."[13] At 10, my daughter, now the very bright and analytical law school graduate, used to ask me to read her the parable at bedtime. I

13. Buttrick, *The Parables of Jesus*, 189.

never asked why, but I knew it spoke to her in some way. The sentiment it engendered may have produced my Father's Day card from her last June. It was a photo of a father, his daughter by the hand. The message read: "For listening any time, for believing every time, for loving me all the time." Speaking of being conquered.

As the world moves away from serious consideration of the old gods of the old religions, away from the lovely but impossible idea that an invisible deity holds all in its hands and will make everything all right somehow, what will become of such stories as the father and his prodigal son?

The father, as Luke depicted him, was the avatar of unconditional love and, more than that, of an aggressive love. His love for his sons—the younger a terminally disrespectful wastrel, the elder an insufferable prig—was entirely independent of their conduct toward each other and toward him. That image must have hovered over the labors of the hymn writer as he paraphrased the Twenty-third Psalm thus: "Perverse and foolish oft I strayed, but yet in love he sought me, and on his shoulder gently laid, and home, rejoicing, brought me."[14]

Of course, the psalmist and the hymnist each were envisioning the biblical deity, the former no doubt in images evoked by some gentle shepherd of his acquaintance, the latter by the psalm itself and of the "good shepherd" appellation associated with Jesus of Nazareth, especially by John the Evangelist (see John 10:11–18). John had already established for kerygmatic purposes the idea of Jesus being the incarnation of God.

Considering the uncritical deference given to the Bible, even by clergy who should know better, it will be difficult to craft a homily on this text while not only observing but practicing intellectual honesty. The placement of Luke 15:11–32 at this place in the liturgical stream of Sundays is a mute appeal by its editors to preach divine forgiveness which the creeds assert came through

---

14. Baker, "The King of Love My Shepherd Is," The Hymnal 1982, p. 645.

the events that will be depicted in the lections over the next three weeks.

The agnostic nonbeliever and the secular humanist will have to be given something of more substance if he or she is to deal with this text. Buttrick's suggestion that it be read without any comment or explanation is not a bad idea, but it would then have to be read as Richard Burton might have read it: movingly and memorably. Failing that, the homilist might treat the story as a large-canvas painting and bid the congregation, as it were, to stand back and regard it both in its parts and as a whole. The homilist, like a knowing docent, can point out this shadow, that shaft of light, etc. He or she might ask the congregation to imagine sights, sounds and smells not accounted for in the story.

It would not be at all inappropriate to focus on Luke's remarkable father-figure and to ask how his demeanor, restraint and generosity might be seen as models for foreign and domestic policy initiatives, of community organization, of civic virtue, of family life. "There was a man who had two sons . . ."

Bibliography

Bacon, Francis. *The Advancement of Learning*. 1605.

Baker, Henry Williams. "The King of Love My Shepherd Is," ca. 1868, The Hymnal 1982, Church Hymnal Corp.

Burns, Robert. "Man Was Made to Mourn." 1784.

Buttrick, George A. *The Parables of Jesus*. Garden City, NY: Doubleday, 1928.

Calvin, John. *Institutes of the Christian Religion (Institutio Christianae religionis)*. 1536.

Cameron, Ron. *The Other Gospels: Non-Canonical Gospel Texts*. Philadelphia: Westminster, 1982.

Cook, Harry T. *Christianity Beyond Creeds*. Clawson, MI: Center for Rational Christianity, 1997.

Crossan, J.D. *Jesus: A Revolutionary Biography*. New York: HarperCollins, 1994.

Crossan, J.D., and Reed, Jonathan L. *In Search of Paul: How Jesus's Apostle Opposed Rome's Empire with God's Kingdom*. New York: HarperCollins 2004.

Dawkins, Richard. *The God Delusion*. U.K.: Bantam, 2006.

Doctorow, E.L. *Reporting the Universe (The William E. Massey Sr. Lectures in the History of American Civilization)*. Cambridge, MA: Harvard University Press, 2003.

Fortunatus, Venantius. "Welcome, Happy Morning" hymn, ca. 590.

Harris, Sam. *The End of Faith: Religion, Terror, and the Future of Reason*. New York: W.W. Norton & Co., 2004.

James, William. *Pragmatism: A New Name for Some Old Ways of Thinking*. New York: Longman Green and Co., 1907.

Jenkins, Philip. *The Next Christendom—The Coming of Global Christianity*. New York: Oxford University Press, 2002.

Josephus, Flavius. *Antiquities of the Jews*, ca. 93–94 CE.

Kloppenborg, John S. *The Formation of Q: Trajectories in Ancient Wisdom Collections (Studies in Antiquity and Christianity)*. Minneapolis: Fortress, 1987.

Mack, Burton. *The Lost Gospel: The Book of Q and Christians Origins*. New York: HarperCollins, 1993.

Bibliography

MacMullen, Ramsay. *Voting About God in Early Church Councils*. New Haven, CT: Yale University Press, 2006.

Maugham, W. Somerset. *Cakes and Ale*. U.K.: William Heinemann Ltd., 1930.

Merriam-Webster's Collegiate Dictionary, Tenth Edition. Springfield, MA: Merriam-Webster, 2001.

Meyers, Carol. *Exodus (New Cambridge Bible Commentary)*. New York: Cambridge University Press, 2005.

North, Frank Mason. "Where Cross the Crowded Ways of Life." #609 in The Hymnal 1982, Church Hymnal Corp.

Pagels, Elaine. *Beyond Belief: The Secret Gospel of Thomas*. New York: Random House, 2003.

———. *The Origin of Satan: How Christians Demonized Jews, Pagans, and Heretics*. New York: Random House, 1995.

Shakespeare, William. "Julius Caesar." 1599.

———. "Hamlet." ca 1599–1601.

Stevenson, Robert Louis. *A Child's Garden of Verses and Underwoods*. 1913.

Wordsworth, William. *Lyrical Ballads*, 1798.

———. "Tintern Abbey," 1798.

Wright, Robert. *The Evolution of God*. New York: Little, Brown and Company, 2009.